RAINBOWS AFTER RAIN

Msgr. Laurence J. Spiteri

Rainbows *after* Rain

Discovering
God's Grace in
Everyday Life

SOPHIA INSTITUTE PRESS
Manchester, New Hampshire

Sophia Institute Press
Box 5284, Manchester, NH 03108
1-800-888-9344
www.SophiaInstitute.com

Sophia Institute Press is a registered trademark of Sophia Institute.

paperback ISBN 979-8-88911-540-3

ebook ISBN 979-8-88911-554-0

Library of Congress Control Number: 2025944806

First printing

CONTENTS

Foreword

I AM DELIGHTED TO write the foreword for Msgr. Laurence Spiteri's latest book, entitled *Rainbows after Rain*. This book makes it very evident that, although Msgr. Spiteri has been at the service of the Holy See here at the Vatican for many years, he has never lost touch with the people of God as a priest; as Pope Francis said on a number of occasions, this is a case when the priest has "the smell of the sheep." He has deep insights due to teaching canonical issues, giving retreats all over the world, and his vast experience of being active in a number of tribunals, beginning in his first year as a priest, and now as a prelate auditor of the Roman Rota, the highest Court of Appeals in the niversal Church.

In this book, comprised of twenty-one rather brief chapters, the author skillfully weaves together the narrative of the life of a person, Jimmy, from the moment of his conception until his natural death. It is an exposition of a life that speaks not only about the natural but also the spiritual growth of a person from the moment of his Baptism to the moment of his natural death.

Msgr. Spiteri emphasizes the fact that we must speak of the whole person. Although behavioral sciences speak about the human development of a person, they fail to take into account the spiritual life of the same person, thereby presenting a truncated understanding of the *entire* person. They focus on the physical, mental, psychological, social, sexual, and academic aspects while ignoring the fact that the same person has a soul that also grows in the spiritual journey that the total person embarks on. Thus, Jimmy is portrayed as a person growing in a human society as well as a person growing in a spiritual society, the Church, whose teachings and guidance illuminate Jimmy's way, helping him to fulfill the ultimate reason for his existence: reaching Heaven.

The author takes into account Jimmy's human development by speaking of the growth of his physical reality, with all of its stages of development, his joys and struggles as a son, a boy, a sibling, an adolescent, a young adult, an academic student, a spouse and father, a breadwinner, a caring friend, a parent who has to deal with diverse family problems and crises, one who has to cope with the death of loved ones, and eventually a grandfather in the process of growing in years and into the sunset of his life. But this is half the story of the life of Jimmy. Thus, the author also speaks about the spiritual development of Jimmy as a person endowed by God with the gift of faith, beginning with receiving the Sacrament of Baptism, thereby becoming a member of the People of God and God's son by adoption, and then Jimmy going on to learn how to pray and grow spiritually, receiving the Sacrament of Penance and Reconciliation, making First Holy Communion, being Confirmed, getting married, living a virtuous life, and being involved in the sacramental life of the Church. Jimmy is presented not only as a teacher to his family members and others who are searching for a deeper relationship with the Lord, but also as a witness to the Catholic Faith by how he lives his life and relates to others.

Ultimately Jimmy must deal with his mortality not simply as an event ending earthly life, but one that opens Jimmy to eternal life. The author cleverly weaves together all of the above elements present in the body and soul of Jimmy. His journey touches the lives of his spouse, Jenny, their children and grandchildren, as well as others they encounter on their way to Heaven.

Msgr. Spiteri draws from the experiences of Jimmy's life journey concrete elements that establish that something wonderful happens on our way to Heaven. The narrative shows the author's keen understanding of a person's life on the way to eternal life.

Raffaele Cardinal Farina, S.D.B.
Cardinal emeritus librarian and archivist
Vatican City

Preface

WHAT DO YOU THINK of when you see a rainbow in the sky? It makes me think of the first rainbow in the Bible, in the familiar story of Noah and the Ark, found in the Book of Genesis. God has decided to send a great Flood to cleanse the earth from humanity's corruption and violence. However, God wants to protect righteous Noah and his family and instructs Noah to build an ark wherein the lives of he, his family, and many varieties of animals would be spared.[1] After the waters subside, God declares to Noah, "I have set my rainbow in the clouds."[2]

The biblical rainbow is a symbol of God's covenant with humanity, assuring Noah and his family that the previous storms and their effects will be replaced by tranquility and a renewal of God's peace with humanity. For those who love and trust God, even today, the rainbow reminds us that God not only rescues us from the storms in our personal life, but that He also remains faithful and never abandons us. He, so to speak, walks down each rainbow's bridge that connects Heaven with earth, and makes His love manifest in our lives until we, at the end of our life, walk that bridge toward Heaven.

It's like the line Phil Collins sings in "Something Happened on the Way to Heaven":

[1] See Gen. 6–9.
[2] Gen. 9:13

Something happened on the way to Heaven/
It got a hold of me and wouldn't let go.[3]

Now, what Phil Collins intended to communicate through these lyrics is probably something very different from how I interpret them. That's okay — this has been done and is being done by the Church through the centuries. From ancient times the Church has given an utterly new and Christian meaning to pagan places and beliefs. Pagan temples were transformed into Catholic churches, and pagan events and customs were sanitized of their pagan aspects in order to assist people in leaving behind the pagan features and abiding by the new Christian understanding and lifestyle. There are at least two events that stand out as being Christianized during the ancient Christian times: the celebration of Christmas in the fourth century and the transformation of the pagan Temple of the Pantheon into a Catholic church early in the seventh. Let's take a look at both of these.

The winter solstice was a special event in the annual cycle for some cultures going back to the Neolithic Period (the final stage of the Stone Age), some ten thousand years before the birth of Jesus Christ. The arrival of the winter solstice indicated the appearance of the shortest day in the year and the beginning of the winter season. What today remain as ancient ruins in the layouts of the archaeological sites of such places as Stonehenge in England and Newgrange in Ireland reveal something interesting: the primary axes of both monuments seem to have been carefully aligned on a sightline pointing to the winter solstice sunrise (Newgrange) and the winter solstice sunset (Stonehenge).

---

[3]   "Something Happened on the Way to Heaven" from *But Seriously*, Atlantic Virgin, 1989, released April 16, 1990, lyrics by Phil Collins and Daryl Stuermer.

The Roman Saturnalia was an ancient Roman festival in honor of the Roman god Saturn. The Saturnalia festival was celebrated on December 17 of the calendar of Julius Caesar (the Julian calendar).[4] Later on, the festivities were expanded to seven days, ending on December 23. Everything was shut down in Rome, including the schools and courts. It was still celebrated in the Roman Empire when Jesus was born.

The holiday was celebrated with a sacrifice at the Temple of Saturn that stood in the Roman Forum, followed by a public banquet, private gift-giving, incessant partying, and a carnival atmosphere that overturned Roman social norms: gambling was permitted, and masters served their slaves at table. But because the celebrations were replete with hedonism and self-indulgence, the Church decided to "baptize" these celebrations, infusing them with Christian meaning and disinfecting them from every immoral and pagan behavior. This radical transformation did not take a long time to implement and was subsequently associated with Jesus Christ, the Light from lights, True God and True Man, the Savior of the world. The Church, in a way, was saying: "Show me a newborn baby, and I will show you Jesus of Bethlehem; point to me a soul, and I will point out to you its Redeemer."

But why do we celebrate Jesus' birth on December 25? St. Hippolytus[5] originally designated December 25 as the date of birth of Jesus early in the third century of Christianity. He based his calculations on the assumption that the conception of Jesus took place at

---

4   Julius Caesar gave Rome a new calendar in 46 B.C., which for all practical purposes remained in effect for about 1,600 years, that is until Pope Gregory XIII (1572–1585) reformed it in 1582 and gave us the calendar most of the world now follows.

5   Hippolytus of Rome (170–235) was the first antipope. He eventually made peace with the Church and died as one of her martyrs.

the spring equinox, which he placed on March 25, and then added nine months. By the middle of the fourth century, the Christian churches in what is now called Western Europe celebrated the birth of Jesus on December 25. This is one of the indications that the Christianization of the pagan festivities moved rather rapidly. The Church also dedicated a number of days to celebrate Christmas. The Christmas Season ended on the Sunday following the Epiphany.

Now, our attention turns to the famous Pantheon, which was transformed into a Catholic church that still stands today. The Greek term *Pantheon* means the "temple of all gods." It was a pagan Roman temple that was consecrated as a Catholic church under the title of the Basilica of St. Mary and the Martyrs in A.D. 609. The original pagan temple was erected on the site of an earlier pagan temple commissioned by Marcus Agrippa (63–12 B.C.), during the reign of Emperor Augustus (27 B.C.–A.D. 14). When this edifice burned down, the Roman emperor Hadrian (A.D. 76–138) rebuilt the temple and probably dedicated it in A.D. 126. Its dome is still the world's largest unreinforced concrete dome, and it remains one of the best-preserved Roman buildings of antiquity. Its original setting has undergone some adjustments, partly due to its continuous use. The famous concrete dome has a circular opening which, to this very day, serves as the main source of natural light for the church.

When the Byzantine emperor Phocas donated the building to Pope Boniface IV (608–615), the Pope converted the pagan temple into a Catholic Church and consecrated it to St. Mary and the Martyrs on May 13, 609. During the consecration ceremony, some twenty-eight cartloads of relics of the martyrs that had been removed from the catacombs were placed in a porphyry basin beneath the consecrated high altar. Thus, instead of razing a pagan temple, the Pope converted it into a Christian temple (church). In so doing, the building was spared abandonment and saved from eventually turning into ruins, as happened to the majority of ancient Roman buildings.

But what is the purpose of "Christianizing" something, whether an object or an idea? The answer is rather simple. It lets the light of Jesus Christ permeate life and culture. It brings Christ's message to the marketplace, that is the personal life of people. In their final report on the twentieth anniversary of the closing of the Second Vatican Council, the International Theological Commission called this approach *inculturation,* which was defined as "the intimate transformation of authentic cultural values through their integration in Christianity in the various human cultures."[6]

Every Catholic at Baptism is commissioned to bring the Lord's message to every aspect of human activity. In other words, Catholics of every generation are called to Christianize the secular world they live in. We are called to be the contemporary light of Christ and chase away the darkness of the secular world and its ephemeral values. We are called to transform what exists by injecting the Lord's message and values, thereby changing people's mentality rather than simple outward appearance. We go to work, but we go there as Christian workers.

I have a young friend, whom I baptized years ago, who now runs his father's company. He instituted a few minutes of prayer and sharing at the beginning of work every day, inviting not only Catholic employees but all his employees. He told me that this practice has really changed things. Employees are more careful with their language, gentler and kinder with one another. The atmosphere at work is very professional, respectful, and peaceful. Their work was transformed from something they had to do simply to earn a living to

---

[6]   International Theological Commission, *Faith and Inculturation* (1988), introduction, no. 3. See also John Paul II, encyclical letter *Slavorum Apostoli,* (June 2, 1985), no. 21.

something dignified. These minutes that they spend praying together at the beginning of each workday have deepened their love for God and the Catholic Church, and the non-Catholic employees have become better persons. Perhaps this love was always there, but this human "spark" soon became a flame.

This young man was a true Catholic missionary in his own "little," but very inspirational, way. Something great happened on his way to Heaven. He reminds me of what St. Basil the Great (330–379), writing to his monks, instructed them to do:

> Love of God is not something that we can be taught. We did not learn from someone else how to rejoice in light or want to live, or to love our parents or guardians … As soon as the living creature (that is, man) comes to be, a power of reason is implanted in us like a seed, containing within it the ability and the need to love. When the school of God's law admits this power of reason, it cultivates it diligently, skillfully nurtures it, and with God's help brings it to perfection.[7]

No one can love God for us, just as no one can breathe for us. It is very personal, intimate, and irreplaceable. However, someone's exemplary lifestyle can move us and others to love God. Even this internal movement is rooted in God's grace.

The purpose of this book is to tell the story of a single family, across several generations, to show how God's activity in each life is shown not just in the time we spend at Mass but all our lives. And it shows how God works through each of us on our journey toward Heaven through "Rainbow Moments" by which we love and inspire

---

[7] St. Basil the Great, *Detailed Rules for Monks*, resp. 2, 1.

those around us. The most important moments of our lives are not restricted to places and moments of prayer and reflection; rather, God invites us to discover Him in every life experience, especially that which seems to be routine and, perhaps, even insignificant.

In the chapters that follow this preface, we are invited to reflect on amazing things that might happen to us on our way to Heaven.

RAINBOWS AFTER RAIN

CHAPTER ONE

A Son Is Given

FROM THE VERY MOMENT of our conception until God calls us to Himself by extinguishing our earthly life, marvelous and amazing things happen to us on our way to Heaven, though they are sometimes cloaked in ordinary events. The first amazing "Rainbow Moment" of God's love comes at the very start of life, when He gives us individually His first gift: the gift of life.

From the first moment of existence, we are created in God's image.[8] He creates us and brings us into being not at some undefined time during our mother's pregnancy, but at the very moment of our conception. God alone was our first witness. Our existence was probably not noticed for a couple of weeks by our mother, much less by our father. Yet, God was fully aware of it from its very first moment.

And as it is with each of us, so it was with Jesus. The earthly life of Christ began at His conception and not at some subsequent time during Our Lady's pregnancy. The Second Person of the Blessed Trinity became man at the moment of His Incarnation. This is something revealed to us, made known to us by God and communicated to us by the gift of the Catholic Faith. It is a core, infallible, unalterable, perennial teaching of the Catholic Church.

---

[8]   Gen. 1:26–27; 5:1; 9:6.

There continues to be much agitation due to the decision of the Supreme Court of the United States in overturning *Roe v. Wade* on Friday, June 24, 2022. Ironically, when the abortion law was in force, pro-abortionists insisted that all must respect *Roe v. Wade*; now that that decision has been overturned they insist that abortion rights must be restored rather than accepting and respecting the law of the land. They have hardened themselves against the truth of the matter: at the moment of conception, a unique and unrepeatable *human* life comes into existence, created by God Himself.

I recently heard a prominent theologian state that the Lord's DNA was created at the moment of His Incarnation. This is a point we don't reflect upon enough as Catholics: the Lord inherited every part of His humanity — body and soul — from Our Lady, who was immaculately conceived. God became a human being at conception (the Annunciation). We profess it in the Creed: "For us men and for our salvation He came down from heaven, and by the Holy Spirit was incarnate of the Virgin Mary, and became man." This is a core doctrine that binds all Catholics, and this is a matter of authentic faith and not secular politics or science. Furthermore, God became man for the sake of the entire humanity and not only for Catholics or other kinds of Christians.

It is at this same moment — the moment of conception — that we are created in the image of God.[9] The truth is not always welcome, and some respond in desperate ways in a moment of personal crisis. Abortion is always murder, and God alone sees the heart of the matter. He will judge justly both the one who commits a one-time terrible and tragic event that does not reflect his or her overall mentality, and those who insist on abortion or the right to abortion for anyone — who deny that the group of "cells" in a

---

[9]   Ibid.

woman's womb from the moment of conception is a real, live human being.

As any mother will tell you, each pregnancy is unique. From the moment the couple becomes aware of their unborn child, that baby begins to make a difference not only in the mother's body and chemistry, but also in the life of other people, especially the father. It is common today that an expectant couple announces: "We are pregnant," though we know full well that only the wife is pregnant. The statement indicates immediately that both parents are involved in the life of the child from the moment pregnancy is discovered. The baby becomes a source of great joy.

Let us call the person "Baby Jimmy." His life, beginning from his conception, serves as a faucet as God's blessings are poured out like water to refresh numerous people, beginning with the parents.

Mothers, just recall the joy when you suspected that you were pregnant, and then the joy when that pregnancy was confirmed. Fathers, just recall seeing the happiness across your wife's face and the reciprocated happiness in you when you were told that a baby is on the way. Very often, parents don't hoard this joy to themselves but share it with others, with grandparents and siblings, with relatives, with neighbors, with friends, and with people at work. The unborn baby's very presence brings great joy.

Yes, it is a fact that some pregnancies carry health risks. And yet the mother's instinct is to protect her baby, to take the necessary measures and precautions to shield this tiny and very vulnerable life growing every moment in her womb.[10] There are many courageous

---

[10] One person who immediately comes to my mind is Gianna Beretta Molla (1922–1962), an Italian Roman Catholic pediatrician. She was the tenth child of fourteen in her original family. As a medical doctor, she was very

and inspiring mothers who ignore the high risk of their pregnancy and insist upon carrying their "Baby Jimmy" to full term.

As his baby grows and he comes to anticipate fatherhood, Baby Jimmy's father becomes very protective of his unborn child in the womb of his wife, of the little person that he will eventually see and hold in his arms. Baby Jimmy's mother begins to be very careful of what she eats and drinks, and of what she does physically — including resting — for her baby's sake. Baby Jimmy's parents also pray and ask others to join them in praying for a healthy pregnancy, a healthy child, and a safe delivery.

In this regard, when we were tiny unborn babies, we too made a difference in others. The gift of life that we received from God at the moment of our conception turns us into the gifts of joy, love, caring, and prayer. Because of us, people were moved from being self-centered or self-absorbed, a least for a short time. Because of us, others changed for the better even before we had seen the light of day, much less uttered a word.

Next, Baby Jimmy's parents experienced the joy of preparing a specific place for him at home. It does not matter what the home is like — large or small, crowded or spare — his parents wanted to create a space full of love and care, a place where their child would experience kindness and encouragement, protection and spiritual nourishment. Baby Jimmy's parents are not afraid their child will judge them for what they have (or have not) acquired; their hearts are full of hopes for what their child will become.

---

much aware of the risks she was taking with her fourth child. Yet, she courageously refused medical intervention that would endanger the life of her baby. In the end, she gave up her life for the sake of the life of her child. She was declared a saint by Pope St. John Paul II on May 16, 2004. Her fourth child, also called Gianna (born April 21, 1962), was present along with her father and three siblings. It was the first time in the history of the Church that a husband witnessed the canonization of his wife.

Slowly they choose a specific place and begin to decorate the baby's room. Homemade or purchased items appear progressively. Next, clothes and bedding arrive. Parents usually opt to pass up something they would like to have or do and instead put aside the money for their baby's future needs. Babies have made a difference in the lives of their parents, siblings, and grandparents.

Some countries have a wonderful tradition to have a "baby shower," a shower of gifts for the yet-to-be-seen baby. People gather together to make this celebration. There is joy, laughter, great company, storytelling, shared information and insight, and festivities. People become altruistic and generous. The focus is on the unborn baby rather than themselves. The baby has made a difference for the better in making people happy, generous, and unselfish.

As the day of his arrival draws near, Baby Jimmy's parents turn their minds to an important question: Who should be his godparents? This can become a rather complicated and very delicate process and might carry the risk of making the non-chosen feel hurt or inadequately appreciated. So, parents might be required to become very diplomatic.

At last, the big day arrives, the day Baby Jimmy will open his eyes on the world! This does not come without cost, especially to the mother. During the natural birthing process, she often experiences excruciating pain! However, that pain has meaning because of the gift she will receive: her own precious child. As we reflect on this birthing pain, we are reminded that all suffering has meaning when we unite our experience to the purpose of the piercing pain of the crucified Lord. This pain, too, was undertaken out of the God's love for the forgiveness of all human sins and as a preparation for our birth in Heaven.

Hours later, Baby Jimmy is born amidst a rush of water and blood. If we just step back for a moment and think about the Church, we might remember that the Church was born out of water and blood flowing from the side of the crucified Lord.[11] In both scenarios, there is a new birth and a new beginning.

[11] John 19:34.

A Rainbow Moment

Even before he is born, Jimmy is making a difference in the spiritual life of his parents and godparents as they receive pre-Baptism instructions regarding the meaning and responsibilities to be willingly assumed at Baby Jimmy's Baptism.

Consider for a moment how your own Baptism was a sign of God's love in the lives of your parents and godparents. Perhaps it was a moment of conversion for them (or for others present at the time), encouraging them to resume their Catholic sacramental life at a deeper level or even return to the practice of the Catholic Faith. Civilly married godparents might have been inspired by the Spirit to enter a sacramental Marriage. Perhaps the invitation to be a "witness" to the Baptism might inspire a non-Catholic "godparent" to take a closer look at the Catholic Faith as a result of participating in the pre-Baptism classes or the actual Baptism ceremony! [12]

Even from the first moments of our existence, the "image of God" is alive in us, calling us to be witnesses to the truth of our faith. How have you experienced this?

---

[12] A non-Catholic, Christian godparent is called a "Christian witness."

CHAPTER TWO

A New Beginning

THE MOMENT A BABY is born, the first thing that the mother, father, and medical personnel look for is a sign of life. The first sound that they want to hear from the newborn is a cry. With his first wail, Baby Jimmy declares to those present and to the rest of the world: "I am here and I am alive!"

Next, Baby Jimmy's body, having been very carefully washed, is professionally examined and declared healthy. Then the baby is handed to his mother, so fingers and toes can be counted, and a prayer of thanksgiving can be whispered.

Now everyone wants to look at Baby Jimmy in excitement and joy. That bundle of joy, wrapped warmly, has elicited change in those around and within the eventual visitors. "Handle with care" is the rule of the day for everyone who approaches Baby Jimmy. Day and night, his cries elicit attention for any number of reasons; he is unaware of either day or night, or whether his parents are exhausted or restful. He is ignorant of his surroundings or who might be present. He continues with his subtle declaration: "I am here and I am alive!"

From the moment of his birth, Baby Jimmy will encounter numerous professionals in the medical field. These professionals will examine Baby Jimmy, answer questions and address concerns of the new parents, diagnose possible illnesses, provide necessary inoculations, and ensure his overall health. And just as his parents consult and discern who is the best doctor for their baby, we too will need spiritual assistance and God's grace when we encounter spiritual illness (sins). We will need to be attended to and healed by the Lord's loving grace and mercy.

✠   ✠   ✠

Sacred Scripture reminds us that the Lord stands ready to heal us, physically and spiritually, when we seek healing from Him. The Psalms speak about it: "God will restore them when they are sick, lying upon their bed of suffering. He will raise them up again and restore them back to health,"[13] and "He heals the wounds of every shattered heart."[14] The prophet Jeremiah assures the faithful, "I will restore you to health and heal your wounds."[15]

Throughout the Gospels, Our Lord healed souls and bodies numerous times during His public ministry. Jesus takes care of the entire person — healing bodies, forgiving sins.[16] After all, Jesus Christ is the Divine Healer. However, we should turn to Him not only when we are physically and spiritually sick, but frequently throughout the day and ask for His assistance and company.

Just as his parents consult others about Baby Jimmy, we also need to consult others about our spiritual health and progress by seeking spiritual advice from a spiritual director who might not only help us in dealing with some spiritual ailment but also propose what might bring about spiritual healing so as to help us grow in holiness. Thus, the small baby has contributed subtly something good by reminding us of the need of God's assistance and that of other spiritually wise persons.

Newborns need to be washed clean, dressed, kept warm, and fed. Only the baby's face is visible the majority of this time, yet we

---

13   Ps. 41:3.

14   Ps. 147:3.

15   Jer. 30:17.

16   See, for example, Matt. 9:1–6; Mark 2:1–12; Luke 5:17–26; John 5:8–18.

know the rest of the body is attached to it. In a way, this is an act of faith, for we take as a real fact that which we do not see. Similarly, this occasion reminds us of faith. St. Paul wrote: "Faith is … the certainty that what we cannot see truly exists."[17]

Just as Baby Jimmy's body is attached to his head, so the Church is attached to "Christ [who] is the head of the Church, which is His body."[18] Each newborn reminds us of a spiritual reality, and something amazing happens on our way to Heaven.

The washing of Baby Jimmy invites us to look at our own soul and determine if it needs to be cleansed through the Sacrament of Penance and Reconciliation so that all the spiritual stains we have acquired up till then will be washed away through God's infinite mercy. No sin, whatever it might be, is out of the reach of God's forgiving love and mercy, and we cannot afford to embark on a silent long decline of inner peace. Then, like the child, our soul will be dressed in the garment of God's compassion and love, and our heart will become warm once again by our flame of love for God and neighbor.

The child cannot fetch nourishment for himself; rather, he cries out for it. Each time Baby Jimmy cries, he indicates with his tone what he needs; he teaches his parents when he needs to be fed, or he is uncomfortable, or it is time to change his diaper. And just as his parents listen carefully to discern what their child needs, so we must learn how to listen to God while we pray. However, if we cannot listen to people whom we see, how can we listen to God whom we do not see?

Baby Jimmy is totally dependent on others, particularly the mother, for nourishment. Similarly, we long for spiritual

17   Heb. 11:1.
18   Col. 1:18.

nourishment, particularly for Holy Eucharist, which the Lord offers to us through Mother Church, as well as His graces. We are completely dependent on God for our spiritual food. We gradually become more and more aware of our need for God in our life. Our cry should come from the deep recesses of our heart for, as St. Augustine said, "Our heart is restless until it rests in You."[19] Pope Francis stated that "In Augustine it was this very restlessness in his heart which brought him to a personal encounter with Christ, brought him to understand that the remote God he was seeking was the God who is close to every human being, the God close to our heart, who was 'more inward than my innermost self.'"[20]

A farmer would tell us that one should not throw a huge amount of water at one time on arid soil; most of it will roll off and take with it the parched soil. Instead, water should be poured slowly and patiently. Even nature itself indicates this; when there are torrential rains, all kinds of things are carried away: terrain, cars, houses, and, tragically, people. Similarly, God sends upon an arid soul the water of grace in a very patient and consistent manner. And one of the ways he does this is through little children — like Baby Jimmy.

Something amazing happens as we encounter helpless, vulnerable souls like this on our way to Heaven, for God uses them as a means to call people gently and consistently back to conversion and more and more reliance on Him. The inspired Psalmist admonished not to put our trust in people with earthly powers (our modern-day version of princes), but in our merciful Lord.[21]

---

[19] St. Augustine, *Confessions*, chap. 1:1.
[20] Francis, Homily at Mass (August 28, 2013), no. 2.
[21] Ps. 60:11; 108:12–13; 118:8–9; 146:3.

A Rainbow Moment

Just as Baby Jimmy's parents know instinctively to "handle baby Jimmy with care," God also holds us in His arms with gentle love and care so that no harm comes to us—if we allow Him to hold us, of course. Baby Jimmy reminds us of the gentleness and protective love of God toward us.

As they first introduce their baby to the world, parents proudly say: "This is our baby." Something similar happens on the spiritual level at the moment of Baptism. God states, "But now, this is what the Lord says—He who created you ... you are Mine."[22] God delights in his Fatherhood, and in the fact that we belong to Him.

Bringing a child home for the first time is a most joyful moment for mother and baby, and for the father, any older siblings, and the extended family. This also points to a spiritual reality: the Church, our loving Mother, takes us to our spiritual family once we have been sacramentally cleansed from sin, both original and personal. There, our brothers and sisters in the Lord on earth and in Heaven welcome us and rejoice with the angels for, as Jesus states: "There is joy in heaven when one sinner repents,"[23] and

---

[22] Isa. 43:3. See also Exod. 19:5–6; Deut. 32:9; Ezek. 16:8.
[23] Luke 15:7.

"There is joy in the presence of God's angels over one repenting sinner."[24]

As he continuously holds and protects us, God also feeds us and is ever mindful of our needs. As the prophet Isaiah declares: "Can a mother forget her infant, be without tenderness for the child of her womb? Even should she forget, I will never forget you!"[25] Furthermore, the inspired Psalmist recalls: "Even if my father and mother abandon me, the Lord will care for me."[26] Thus, when we feel downcast, let us remember the Lord's reassuring ways—God never forgets His children, Jesus never forgets His brothers and sisters, and Our Lady never forgets her sons and daughters.

Thus, even as we observe the loving and simple act of a mother nursing a baby, we are reminded of all the amazing gifts God gives us on our way to Heaven.

[24] Luke 15:10.
[25] Isa. 49:15, NAB.
[26] Ps. 27:10.

CHAPTER THREE

Chosen by God

DUE TO OUR ADVANCED modern technology in the world of medicine, parents can choose to know the gender of their baby during a pregnancy. Others choose to be surprised when the baby is born. In either case, parents usually begin to think of a name for their baby at some stage during pregnancy. The name is carefully selected and, at times, done very diplomatically, for a variety of reasons.

Some might choose the name of a recently deceased loved one. Others might choose a name of a parent or grandparent. Until recently, many parents in Latin countries chose the name of the saint of the day on which the baby was born or the name of a saint to whom they are devoted or through whose intercession they prayed to be given the gift of a child. Others might choose a name for sentimental reasons.

Choosing a baby's name is very important because he will carry this name all his life. Some parents choose an unusual name without thinking about how it will impact the child. The name will enter the registration of baby's birth certificate, the census, legal documents such as a passport or driver's license, all kinds of school and medical records, the church sacramental registry, legal documents of ownership of all kinds of property and contracts, and finally, the death certificate. The name is usually inscribed on the tombstone.

A person's name provides us with access to that person's attention, reference, and memory. We refer to a person by name when speaking to him or talking about him. We use names to look up phone numbers to call people or addresses to contact them. We recall a deceased person's name when we speak or write about the deceased person. Thus, a person's name is essential for personal identity.

The naming of a child invites us to a spiritual reflection. For the sake of consistency, let us continue to state that the parents named their child "Jimmy." Sacred Scripture contains numerous references to God either giving a name to a baby in the womb or knowing the name. I will make reference only to a few.

In the Old Testament, the Lord instructed Abraham to name his son by Sarah "Isaac."[27] The prophet Isaiah reminds his countrymen that God called Jacob and Israel by name: "Thus says the LORD … I have called you by name."[28] He reminds his people that God "has engraved your name on the palm of My hands"[29] and, regarding himself, "The LORD called me from the womb; from the body of my mother, He gave me my name."[30]

In the New Testament, St. Joseph was instructed to give the name of Jesus to Mary's son once He was born.[31] The Archangel Gabriel instructed Zachariah to name his son "John."[32] All of us are familiar with the scenes of the Lord calling His Apostles by name as He invited them personally to follow Him.[33] We might also note that no name was given when someone turned down the Lord's invitation to follow Him, as was the case with the rich young man[34] or the one whom Jesus invited but who wanted to go home first to give a

27 Gen. 17:19, 21.
28 Isa. 43:1.
29 Isa. 49:16.
30 Isa. 49:1.
31 Matt. 1:21; Luke 1:31; 2:21.
32 Luke 1:13, 63.
33 Matt. 4:18-22; Mark 3:16–20; Luke 5:1-11; John 1:35–51.
34 Matt. 19:21–22; Mark 10:21–22; Luke 18:21–23.

farewell to his family,[35] or the cured possessed man who wanted to follow Jesus but was told to do otherwise.[36] Finally, there is that beautiful passage from the Gospel of St. John when Jesus reminds us that He calls us by name: "The sheep [all of us] hear His [the Lord's] voice, and He calls His own sheep [us] by name."[37]

It is not by some coincidence or happenstance that God calls each of us, His adopted children, by name. St. Paul reminds the Christians of Ephesus that "God chose us in Christ before the world was established."[38] We are not Catholics by some accident, for the Lord invites us to "rejoice that your names are written in heaven"[39] and registered in the Book of Life.[40] Moreover, your name and mine are engraved in the palm of God's hand.[41] It is a permanent inscription that will never be erased!

Perhaps, one of these nights, we should look at the sky and pray: "Lord, thank You for writing my name up there." When naming a newborn baby makes us recall these beautiful things, then something amazing happens on our way to Heaven.

The Baptism day of Baby Jimmy is a celebration his entire family will always remember; it marks his spiritual birthday as a member of the household of God.[42] At his Baptism, Baby Jimmy becomes a messenger of God's invitation to parents and godparents to either deepen their

---

35   Matt. 8:21–22; Luke 9:59–60.
36   Mark 5:18-19; Luke 8:38-39.
37   John 10:3.
38   Eph. 1:4.
39   Luke 10:20.
40   Phil. 4:3.
41   Isa. 49:16.
42   Eph. 2:19 calls the Baptized "members of God's household, the church of the living God." See also 1 Tim. 3:15.

Christian commitment or reform their lives. This is a gift that might be easily overlooked.

What other graces does the Lord provide to Baby Jimmy's parents, family, and friends who participate at his Baptism? First of all, the parents are provided with the opportunity of choosing godparents. The law of the Church (Canon Law) gives these specifics:

> Parents are obliged to take care that infants are baptized in the first few weeks; as soon as possible after the birth or even before it, they are to go to the pastor to request the sacrament for their child and to be prepared properly for it....
>
> ... there must be a founded hope that the infant will be brought up in the Catholic religion.[43]

We should note that there is no reference as to whether the parents are married in church, civilly married, or not married. On the other hand, there are specific conditions set for godparents:

✣ When there are two sponsors, there must be one male and one female.

✣ The sponsors must have the disposition to fulfill their responsibility.

✣ Godparents must be at least sixteen years of age and have received the Sacraments of the Eucharist and Confirmation and be Catholics in good standing.

✣ The baby's parents cannot also be the godparents.

---

[43] *Code of Canon Law* (henceforth CIC), c. 867 §1; c. 868 §1 , in *Code of Canon Law: Latin- English Edition* (Washington, DC: Canon Law Society of America, 1999).

One of the sponsors may be a baptized non-Catholic, called a witness, if there is a second sponsor who is a qualified Catholic.[44] Furthermore, parents and sponsors are to undertake a course of instruction on the meaning of Baptism and what responsibilities it entails.[45] Thus, once again Baby Jimmy provides a wonderful opportunity for parents and godparents to deepen their understanding and commitment to the Catholic Faith — a moment of conversion.

One might ask, Why should a baptized non-Catholic witness also promise to look after the Catholic spiritual growth of a child? Well, I know of many baptized non-Catholic parents who are highly diligent in bringing their child to Mass on Sundays and Holy Days, taking their child to religious instruction in preparation to receive a sacrament, and paying for the child's tuition at a Catholic educational institution. In other words, such a parent assists the child in traveling the journey to Heaven as a Catholic.

Baby Jimmy's Baptism reminds each person present that each of us, individually, is called by God to be a Catholic, but this divine choice is never based on merit or mere custom ("Our family has always been Catholic"). It is a matter of Divine Providence, which shows itself through the centuries.

Since Jesus Christ personally established the Church, He also calls each and every one of us to follow Him. You and I are called, individually and personally, to be not only Christian but specifically to be *Catholic.* It is not some impersonal or flippant calling or invitation. Jesus chooses each one of us to be and to live as His brother or sister. The Lord calls us to be His modern-day apostles and witnesses. On

---

[44]   *CIC,* cc. 872–874.
[45]   *CIC,* c. 851, §2.

the other hand, all other Christians, and indeed every person, will be held responsible according to the spiritual calling he or she has received from God.

When we plan to travel overseas, we need a passport. This passport identifies us as being citizens of a specific country. It does not only enable us to travel but also to enter and experience a somewhat different part of the world we have read about or heard of. Similarly, the preparations involved in readying the parents and godparents for the Baptism of Baby Jimmy provide them with the opportunity of recalling that life on earth is also a spiritual journey to Heaven, a place that we cannot see in earthly measured existence — and yet we need a passport to travel there, something that identifies us as being citizens of Heaven.

Just as we never cease to be the children of our parents in measured time, so we do not cease to be children of God in eternity. Thus, at Baptism God provides us with another kind of passport, another spiritual rather than civil identity. It is stamped by the finger of God and declares that our citizenship is that of Heaven,[46] for we are "fellow citizens with the saints and members of the household of God."[47] The passport identifies us as baptized children of God and the stamp is the permanent and eternal seal of God on our soul. This spiritual passport reminds us that we live in a passing foreign land, the world, for our true country is Heaven.[48]

Therefore, Baby Jimmy's Baptism reminds us of the day that we, too, were "sealed" with a kind of spiritual passport as a member of the Catholic Church. We are part of a community of believers. We all know that the Church wrestles with the violent waves of the inclement ocean of worldly things that buffet around us with ephemeral

---

[46] Eph. 2:19; Phil. 3:20.
[47] Eph. 2:19.
[48] 1 Pet. 2:11.

promises, scandals, corruption, betrayals, contempt, prejudice, defections, malfeasance, counterfeit teachings, unfounded accusations, and demoralizing attacks from within and outside the Church. However, we should never be surprised, for the Catholic Church has experienced this from her very beginning.

A Rainbow Moment

Part of the good news is that although there are times when individuals at all levels of the Church succumb to sin and weakness, they are never rejected or abandoned when they genuinely seek God's mercy. Instead, they are forgiven and welcomed back with open arms and, hopefully, their soul will find rest. This is manifestly portrayed in the Parable of the Prodigal Son.[49] Note that when an errant son or daughter returns to the Catholic Church, the person is never re-baptized for the simple reason that the spiritual identity remains forever. This is God's promise to us, something amazing that happens on our way to Heaven.

---

[49] Luke 15:11–32.

New Birth

POPE FRANCIS REMINDED FAMILIES that "By the grace of the sacrament [of Marriage], God makes it a wonderful journey, to be undertaken together with him and never alone. The family is not a lofty ideal that is unattainable in reality. God solemnly promises his presence in your marriage and family, not only on the day of your wedding, but for the rest of your lives. And he keeps supporting you, every day of your journey."[50]

At Baptism, God extends this support not only to the two souls joined in Matrimony, but to their children as well. When the Holy Spirit descends upon on the soul of a child at Baptism, in that moment the child is spiritually washed, cleansed, and sealed forever as belonging to the family of God.[51]

In the course of his lifetime, Baby Jimmy will receive countless baths or showers. However, this sacramental cleansing of Baptism reminds us of God's loving promptness to cleanse us from our spiritual filth caused by sin, whether Original Sin or subsequent personal sins. Pope Francis, during his first Angelus address, stated: "Do not

---

[50] Francis, Address at X World Meeting of Families: Festival of Families (June 22, 2022), no. 1.

[51] Since Baptism may not be repeated, Christ left us another means of having our soul cleansed of the personal (and social) sins we commit as fragile human beings. It is the Sacrament of Penance (Reconciliation).

forget this: the Lord never tires of forgiving! It is we who tire of asking forgiveness."[52] This is wonderful indeed!

As part of the rite of Baptism, the minister includes the "prayer of exorcism," asking the Lord to free Baby Jimmy from Original Sin and for the Holy Spirit to dwell within him and provide him with spiritual strength throughout his life. Some question why an innocent child is born with the stains of a sin that the baby himself is incapable of committing. Why should this child — and every child except for Our Lord and Our Lady — pay the price for a sin committed by our first parents, Adam and Eve?[53]

The truth is that innocent people often suffer due to other people's wicked acts. For instance, when an arsonist starts a fire in a forest, the innocent suffering spreads rapidly: the forest, the vegetation, the possessions, and perhaps even lives of innocent people will go up in flames and smoke. If the fire is huge enough, it is not only the local place that will suffer, but also the atmosphere around the world. Innocent people and nature suffer the consequences from the very personal wicked act of one human being.

All of creation suffers the consequences of the first (Original) sin. The Book of Genesis begins with the beauty of the earth and the universe.[54] After the Fall and the repentance and punishment of Adam and Eve, God does not discard either humanity or His entire creation. Instead of destroying them, God promises to rescue both humans and the rest of creation. The purpose of this rescue operation embraces all that had fallen. The Bible speaks about the accomplishment of this rescue as being the creation of a "new

---

[52] Francis, Angelus (March 17, 2013).
[53] Gen. 3:1–13.
[54] Gen. 1:3–2:3.

heavens and a new earth."[55] It is not simply restricted to "a new humanity," fallen humanity being replaced by a new one.[56]

It is of interest to note that the opening of the Bible, the Book of Genesis, begins with the proclamation that God created the heavens and the earth and all they contain, and ends with the proclamation in the Book of Revelation that the same God will create a new Heaven and a new earth. Why is this so? Because all creation, except for angels, suffers from the consequences of Original Sin.

At Baby Jimmy's Baptism, his parents and loved ones are entrusted with his well-being, and with making sure that the world he grows up in is one that is healthy and fruitful rather than abused and falling apart. In a similar way, the parents, godparents, and the entire Church are entrusted with the spiritual well-being of Baby Jimmy and with making sure he grows in an atmosphere of spiritual health and well-being.

From the moment of Baptism, the loving and caring God cuddles Baby Jimmy, making him feel loved and secure, as Baby Jimmy begins his spiritual journey toward Heaven as an adopted child of God. The same is true for all of us.

As we bear witness to the Baptism of this young soul, we are reminded of this wonderful spiritual life we have all embarked upon, beginning with our own Baptism. At Baptism the Holy Spirit comes to dwell within our souls, marking the beginning of our journey toward Heaven. God then begins to consistently provide

---

[55] Isa. 65:17; 66:22; 2 Pet. 3:13; Rev. 21:1.

[56] In his encyclical *Laudato sí*, Pope Francis wrote of every human being's responsibility to protect our common home. A few years later, he also wrote to the Catholic members of the COP26 meeting in Glasgow, Scotland, on November 9, 2021, that "Time is running out; this occasion must not be wasted, lest we have to face God's judgment for our failure to be faithful stewards of the world he has entrusted to our care."

us with the means of going to dwell in His eternal home. The cost of this "ticket" for this spiritual journey was the Lord's suffering and death. This great sacrifice proved, for all time, God's bountiful love and mercy for us as individuals and as a community of faith; indeed, toward all humanity.

At his Baptism, Baby Jimmy's parents and godparents, as well as all those present, are reminded that they have pledged to teach him how to use this ticket,[57] and that our means of travel is the Church. Our traveling documents are those of Baptism, Confirmation, Confession, the Eucharist, and the other sacraments, according to our state of life. We do not presume, but we are certain that the Church, our pilot, will make safe our journey to Heaven, for the Holy Spirit has been given to her as her Guide and Protector.[58] After all, St. Paul tells the Christians of Thessalonica: "this is the will of God: your sanctification."[59]

✠　✠　✠

Following the homily and Prayers of the Faithful, the minister of Baptism anoints Baby Jimmy on the breast by tracing the Sign of the Cross with the Oil of Catechumens, the oil of salvation in Christ. This oil was used in ancient times on those who were studying to become Catholic (catechumens), indicating that they were being set apart for Baptism. This anointing reminds us that we, too, have been set apart by God to become His adopted sons and daughters. It reminds all of us, including the baptizing minister, that we have been called personally by God. After the blessing of the baptismal waters, all those present are called to renew their own

---

[57] Vatican Council II, Dogmatic Constitution on the Church *Lumen gentium* (November 21, 1964), no. 11; Vatican Council II, Pastoral Constitution on the Church in the Modern World *Gaudium et spes* (December 7, 1965), no. 3; *Catechism of the Catholic Church* (CCC) 2221, 2223, 2225; John Paul II, apostolic exhortation *Familiaris consortio* (November 22, 1981), no. 21.

[58] John 14:16, 26; 15:26; 16:7.

[59] 1 Thess. 4:3.

Baptism vows, to reject Satan and evil, and to profess once again their faith so that they can bring up Baby Jimmy in the Catholic Faith.

Pope Francis has stated that "My word of encouragement is precisely this: start from where you are, and, from there, try to journey together: together as couples, together in your families, together with other families, together with the Church."[60] Thus, one might say that the Baptism ceremony is a subtle challenge to the parents and godparents: declare who you really are, a child of God and a member of the household of God (the Church), and live what you declare. Once again, Baby Jimmy becomes a means of reminding us who we are and how we ought to live. This might be a moment of conversion for adults and the child, bringing them all back to God.

After Baby Jimmy is Baptized with water in the name of the Father, and of the Son, and of the Holy Spirit, the crown of his head is anointed with the Oil of Chrism, recalling how Christ was anointed priest, prophet, and king. Now the child is anointed as a priest, granted access to God's presence through prayer; as a prophet, to proclaim God's divine message in word and by a concrete holy lifestyle as the prophets of old did; and as king, to rule over the darkness of sin with God's help. The minister then challenges all present to "become holy yourselves in every aspect of your conduct, after the likeness of the Holy One who called you; remember, Scripture says, 'Be holy, for I am holy.'"[61] Thus, those present at Baptism are reminded to reflect on how they are personally living out their high calling, their consecration to God. Once again, there is a call for conversion.

After Baby Jimmy's anointing with the Oil of the Chrism, there is the clothing with a white garment. We all know that a child does not wear a garment for long before it is soiled. The parents then wash

---

60   Francis, Address at X World Meeting of Families: Festival of Families (June 22, 2022).

61   1 Pet. 1:15–16.

it clean so that the baby will wear it again. After Baptism, Baby Jimmy is given a white garment which is an outward sign of the purity of his soul. It is a garment that he is admonished to keep clean as he grows older and throughout his life. However, all of us are the sons and daughters of fallen humanity. So we soil our spiritual garment with our personal sins. The garment needs to be washed clean through the Sacrament of Penance and Reconciliation. Every time we have our sins sacramentally forgiven, we put on once again this totally clean white garment, and God is never tired of washing clean our garment, for He is a loving, merciful, and patient God. Through the bestowal of the white garment on the newly baptized baby, those who are participating in the Baptism ceremony are reminded of the need to have their spiritual garment frequently washed clean by God.

Then comes the reminder to all those present that we are called to be the light of Christ in the darkness of the fallen world and all its alluring promises. This is especially true nowadays when life is full of, among many things, anxiety; fear; injustice, wars among nations; the insane threat of usage of nuclear bombs; the selling and buying of arms; local, national, and international discord; abuse of the poor, the marginalized, and those who are in search of a better life; and the abuse of nature and dignity of workers. Being the light of Christ does not only mean that persons and organizations say, write, and agree in words to strive to be just, peaceful, honest, and kind. Words are cheap. Rather, these words must take flesh in action. The Baptism candle, which is lit from the Easter (Paschal) Candle, is given to a parent or godparent in the name of Baby Jimmy, but the exhortation is not only meant for him but for all participating in the Baptism ceremony.

Then comes the short ceremony of the baptizing minister to make the Sign of the Cross on Baby Jimmy's ears and mouth, using the Aramaic word *Ephphatha*, meaning "be opened." All of us have physical ears to hear with and a mouth to speak with. Similarly, we have spiritual ears and mouth that enable all baptized to hear words that come from God.

A Rainbow Moment

St. Paul, in writing to the Christians in Thessalonica, said: "We thank God constantly that in receiving His message from us you took it, not as the word of men, but as it truly is, the word of God at work within you who believe."[62] These words are to be proclaimed not only with words, but by the impact of holy and virtuous deeds. Inherently, we are invited to ask ourselves if we are putting these things into action, if they are shaping our lifestyle as Catholics. Each time we are called upon to witness the Baptism of another young soul, it becomes an occasion for us to evaluate our personal lives, whether God is calling us to deeper conversion. Thus, another amazing thing happens on every person's journey to Heaven.

62 1 Thess. 2:13.

CHAPTER FIVE

The Life Journey Begins

As he develops and grows, Baby Jimmy is the delight not only of his parents, siblings, grandparents, and his extended family, but also of their friends. There are smiles and chuckles as he begins to respond to his name. His first word is followed by small phrases, then longer and more complicated speech. First he acquires the ability to sit up, then crawl on the floor; he begins to grab objects, "cruise" around furniture, and finally take his first independent steps. He graduates from drinking just milk to eating soft food, and then more solid fare. Each day brings highs and lows, endless diaper and clothing changes, teething pains, and little bumps and falls as he progresses from infancy to toddlerhood.

It is a very slow but absolutely necessary process. Family members, especially parents, follow Baby Jimmy's development with the eye of a hawk. Their days are full of visits to the pediatrician, trips to the store, endless laundry, and many nights spent in either making Baby Jimmy go to sleep or lulling him back to sleep. The developing baby keeps the parents very busy, very tired, and occasionally concerned, but most of the time is a great delight and a source of abundant joy.

The developmental growth of a little person should remind us that we, as Catholics, undergo stages of spiritual growth. The baptized baby delights the spiritual family which also encompasses the community of saints in Heaven. We are reminded that God calls us by name, and when God calls, we should hear His voice and focus our attention on Him. We move from being nourished by the milk of knowing the tenets of our Faith to the soft nourishment of slowly understanding what they entail. Baby Jimmy is taught, most probably by the mother or grandmother, to make the Sign of the Cross, to kiss a picture of Jesus and pictures depicting other Saints, especially Our Lady, and eventually to pray the Our Father and the Hail Mary. While teaching these prayers, their teachers are also praying them.

Baby Jimmy's development reminds us that we have received the gift of the Holy Spirit and, therefore, call God "*Abba*, Father."[63] We might smile when we reflect on the great and wonderful blessings the doting God has bestowed upon us. Eventually, our prayer life goes from repeating prayers by heart to speaking directly to God in seeking His protection and love, in thanking Him, in praising Him, and in silently adoring Him. We reach out to grab fervent prayers of petition in faith. We begin to distinguish between and understand good and evil. We experience spiritual teething when our prayers are not answered according to our expectations and perhaps even shed disappointed tears to show how important to us are the things we are asking for. God is there to comfort us, to help us realize that He truly cares about us,[64] and to assist us in realizing that His plan goes beyond today and tomorrow because it deals with eternity.[65] We are reminded that God helps us to take the spiritual first steps that will lead us to walk with Him on earth hand-in-hand until He brings us to the gates of Heaven.

[63] Rom. 8:15.
[64] Matt. 6:26.
[65] Isa. 55:8.

Whereas civil law dictates what is criminal and what is not criminal, God reveals to us what is good and what is evil, thereby not only teaching us the virtuous life but also to avoid sin, as Jimmy learns how to avoid very hot and harmful objects. We become more and more aware that God watches over us in life in a way that goes way beyond the vigilant eye of a hawk. Baby Jimmy's stages of development remind us that God not only comes to our rescue but also comforts us when we feel lost and lack direction; when we feel lonely, lost, unloved, or confused. In those moments, we can hear God's gentle voice of forgiveness and mercy. Each time we stop walking with God and fall into sin,[66] our loving God searches for us to hug us with His mercy and compassion and embrace us as His children.[67] Unlike even the most loving parents, God never tires of attending to our needs. God's love is never exhausted.

As Baby Jimmy grows to toddlerhood, he acquires some independence. He goes to places that are outside the parameters set by his parents, says or repeats words or things that should not be said or repeated, and takes things that should remain untouched.

In all these things, Toddler Jimmy also reminds us of our spiritual development. When we reach the age of reason, we begin to distinguish between good and evil. We might be in the company of others who are not good, whose behavior is sinful, who lie easily and frequently, whose words are simply bad or uncharitable, whose actions lead to trouble. We sin. Granted, these are mostly not huge but small sins, but nevertheless they are sins, for we offend our loving God. We run the risk of moving toward major sins.

---

[66] Francis, Angelus (March 17, 2013).
[67] Luke 15:11–32.

We hear now and again of children who are always in trouble, who steal, who lie all the time, who curse, who blame others for something they did, who are mean to others, who are bullies, who assault and even murder other people. God, no matter what we have done or said, will always forgive us. He will carry us in our fragility. We are reminded that no matter how terrible a sin happens to be, it never falls outside the mercy of God. So we should genuinely seek forgiveness from God and rectify the harm we have done, for we remain accountable for our misdeeds.

As a toddler, Jimmy comes to know the power of the word no, and as a child frequently declares, "This is mine." It is always amazing that one of the very first words a toddler learns and seems to understand is no. One of Jimmy's parents might want to bathe or dress or feed him, and the answer is a very stubborn no to the point of emphasizing the answer with wailing. Or he might claim things which belong to others but insist, "This is mine," holding on to the object in a tug of war that ends with howling.

A Rainbow Moment

Do not these acts remind us of our own reactions to God in our spiritual life? We seem to be averse to God responding no to some specific request which we fervently and persistently have made and continue to make, though we pray in the Our Father: "Your will be done on earth!" Do we not sometimes envy other people's closeness to God and want Him to be very close to us as if we see this intimacy as some kind of trophy and something that we have not worked on because we neglect our life of prayer and fail to live the works of mercy? Thus, we become envious or jealous of other people's spiritual relationship with God while having no real intention to change our ways, because we expect God to deal with us in just the same way as He deals with such people.

Is it not amazing that a toddler's and a child's behavior can be an opportunity to remind us of our spiritual relationship with God and other people and challenge us to walk with God? Truly, if this takes place, then something amazing happens on our journey to Heaven.

CHAPTER SIX

Growth and Moral Choices

WHEN YOUNG JIMMY IS seven years old, he will reach the age of reason. In the meantime, there are new challenges and responsibilities that will form him and give him the basis to know right from wrong.

Jimmy is growing intellectually, emotionally, and socially. Even when he is still very young, his parents expect changes in his behavior, both at home and in school. He is expected to learn to sit still and listen and show respect to his parents and others. He is expected to clean up any messes he makes, and to try to keep clean his room and lend a hand in house chores; he learns to share toys, and to obey without whining or throwing a temper tantrum. He begins to distinguish between good and bad behavior; to play fairly with other children, especially his younger siblings; to get along; to avoid doing or saying bad things; to keep clean his clothes; to avoid mischievous behavior; not to be rude or selfish; and so forth.

Of course, Jimmy learns to fulfill these expectations gradually, based on his age and maturity. It is a time when he needs both firmness and patience, rather than harsh words and discouraging demands, which could cause great frustration and acting out. Jimmy learns to value telling the truth, even when it is not complimentary. This development also has a spiritual counterpart which is offered to parents, family members, and friends.

✠   ✠   ✠

When we reach the age of reason, we start distinguishing between what is good and what is bad, though many people nowadays do not want to call the latter evil! To put it in moral and theological terms: we distinguish between virtue and sin. We receive religious instruction in preparation for our First Confession and our First Holy Communion. Alas, many times young people stop studying and growing in the understanding of our marvelous Faith, as if there is no need of maturing in our spiritual life as we mature in our intellectual or professional life. I am always amazed when I meet a sharp professional who has a child's level of knowing and understanding of the Catholic Faith, although there are religious classes for adults for the offering.

✠   ✠   ✠

Jimmy's preparation for his First Confession reminds us how important it is to turn frequently to the Lord, Who tells us: "You are forgiven. Go and sin no more." In other words, the Lord tells us that He gives us another chance to cooperate with His grace and to become purified and holy.

The Sacrament of Penance and Reconciliation is powerful, beautiful, and wonderful. Through it, with our proper internal disposition, we are forgiven and cleansed — we receive a new chance every time we celebrate this sacrament! Furthermore, the sacrament reminds us of our own need to forgive. God has no memory of forgiven sins. We are to forgive others in a similar fashion, as we are reminded in the Our Father: "Forgive us our trespasses as we forgive those who trespass against us." Thus, we undertake a new beginning in our relationship with God and people.

The Sacrament of Baptism forgives all sins, that is Original Sin and all personal sins a person knowingly and willfully commits before being baptized. But, as we all know from our own personal life, being baptized does not make us immune to sin. Our frail and sin-prone human nature is not changed by simply being baptized. Hence, sins committed after Baptism are forgiven through the reception of the Sacrament of Penance and Reconciliation. Just as a growing baby needs to be bathed frequently, so our heavenly Father has provided the Sacrament of Penance and Reconciliation to make us clean again each time our souls are in need of cleansing.

Keep in mind that this sacrament calls the contrite penitent[68] to an authentic conversion.[69] Our first conversion took place at Baptism, and yet we are also called to an ongoing, second conversion — a lifelong call that requires adherence more and more to the Lord so that we can join St. Paul when he declared: "Christ lives in me."[70] Thus, the sacrament involves much more than simply being the ordinary means to have sins forgiven.[71]

When we reach the age of reason, we should start going to Confession, for it is then that we are capable of making good and bad choices. When we have committed a grave sin, we should express our sorrow to God and go to Confession as soon as possible so as to be sacramentally absolved. Perhaps parents forget that when they stay away from Confession, they are most probably making their children also stay away because there is no one to drive them over to church to confess. Furthermore, it is a concrete inspiration for children seeing their parents going to Confession.

There are many times when the devil tries to dissuade us from going to Confession because we tend to commit the same sins,

---

[68] See Ps. 51:17; John 6:44; 12:32; 1 John 4:10.

[69] Mark 1:15.

[70] Gal. 2:20.

[71] *Lumen gentium*, no. 8.

despite our good intentions. The devil wants us to say: "Why bother? After all, they are the same sins."

Let us reflect on this when dealing with our personal hygiene. We wash ourselves frequently. We do not say that because we are going to get dirty again, we simply do not bother to wash the body. This might lead to a very serious or deadly illness. The same applies to our spiritual life and the forgiveness of our sins.

So how many times should we wash our soul with the Lord's mercy and forgiveness? As many times as is needed. There was a royal saint who used to give alms to the poor. One day, one of her assistants told her that some of those people were going back to the end of the line and ending up with two servings. The saint was not disturbed; she saw no problem, for she always went begging to the Lord for forgiveness of the same sins. What would happen if she was not allowed to go back?

Remember that the Lord always gives us the alms of His mercy and forgiveness, no matter how many times we ask for them, and no matter if they are big or small. These spiritual alms come to us through the Church. Pope St. John XXIII, in his opening address of the Second Vatican Council on October 11, 1962, said, "The Spouse of Christ prefers to use the medicine of mercy rather than the weapons of severity. . . . [the Church is] the most loving mother of all, kind, patient, and moved by mercy and goodness."[72]

✠   ✠   ✠

Jimmy is preparing to make his First Confession before his First Holy Communion. This first experience is important, for we should all receive this sacrament as frequently as possible — and avoid becoming scrupulous of things that are not sinful: for example, thoughts and

---

[72] Pope John XXIII, *Gaudet Mater Ecclesia* (October 11, 1962), no. 17.

sensations that are temptations rather than sins. If one experiences an unwanted blasphemous thought, he need not conclude that the devil has overtaken his soul, or that he has committed a mortal sin. Rather, he must firmly reject the thought and turn to the Lord, filling his thoughts with the goodness and mercy of his Creator.

When Jimmy makes his First Confession and First Holy Communion, he reminds us of the gift we have received in these sacraments. He provides us with the occasion of not only returning to the Lord, but also of being nourished by the Lord in that He gives us Himself as our nourishment.

Jimmy's First Holy Communion elicits in many people the remembrance of the joy and excitement they had when they received the Eucharistic Lord for the first time. I know many Catholic adults who keep a photo of when they received the Lord in the Eucharist for the first time.

Why is the Eucharist so important to Catholics? The Catholic Church was established so that the Lord may personally walk with each of us and nourish us on our personal life journey. Jesus is not only personally present "in spirit," but He remains with us in His fullness: Body, Blood, Soul, and Divinity. This kind of existence is called the Real Presence — the Holy Eucharist.[73] Jesus personally established the Sacrament of Holy Eucharist during the Last Supper in the Upper Room on the night before He died for us on the Cross.[74] He did it so He could remain with us always.

---

[73] The Catholic Church teaches that the words of Consecration of the bread and wine transform them into Jesus Christ Himself, though without changing the outward appearances and taste of the bread and wine. It is called *transubstantiation* because the substances of bread and wine, their inner reality, are changed into Jesus Christ, when He becomes present in His Body, Blood, Soul, and Divinity.

[74] Matt. 26:17–29; Mark 14:12–25; Luke 22:7–20; 1 Cor. 11:23–26.

Does anything exclude us from Holy Eucharist? Only grave or mortal sin—for which Jesus has provided the healing medicine through the Sacrament of Penance. This sacrament cleanses the truly repentant sinner of all sins committed and contritely confessed; Reconciliation enables us to receive once more the Holy Eucharist, the heart and the summit of the life of the Church. Just as it is for Jimmy, so it is for each of us: each time we prepare our hearts to receive all the graces the Lord wants to give us in Holy Communion, something amazing happens on our way to Heaven.

A Rainbow Moment

The Eucharist is called the "Sacrament of Sacraments," for in the Eucharist, the Lord links all the members of His Church to the one sacrifice of the Cross from whence the graces of salvation are showered upon all the members of His Church on earth.[75] Furthermore, when we receive Holy Eucharist we are declaring that we fully abide, not partially but *fully*, by what the Catholic Church officially professes and teaches. Consequently, the reception of Holy Eucharist is not only a proclamation regarding the Real Presence of the Lord, but also a declaration of our Catholic Faith.

If a child does not get enough food, he becomes weak and sick from malnutrition. In a similar way, when we deny ourselves the graces of the Eucharist—either by receiving the Sacrament in an unworthy manner, or by staying away from Mass altogether—our soul becomes weak and sick. We should receive the Eucharist as frequently as we can. Holy Eucharist makes us strong in our faith, helps us to resist temptation to sin, and provides us with the necessary spiritual strength on our journey to eternal life.

[75] CCC 1324–1327.

CHAPTER SEVEN

Adjustment Challenges

JIMMY CONTINUES TO GROW and develop beyond childhood to boyhood, developing on the intellectual level through his studies and the use of personal intellectual talents. Childhood tantrums are no longer tolerated. Rather, control over emotions and signs of genuine respect toward others are expected. Jimmy soon discovers that disrespecting, ignoring, or fighting with his good friends makes their number gradually diminish. He is expected to be not only more good-mannered and sociable, but to meet his gradually increasing responsibilities. Jimmy is progressively aware that he is now accountable not only to his parents, family, and teachers, but also to his friends.

The emergence of adolescence, the next stage of his development, is very challenging and could be very dramatic. Older people used to define this stage as "the difficult years." It would seem that all concerned might be walking on a minefield, and things might blow up at any time.

Just as we do not stop developing physically, emotionally, intellectually, and socially, we should not stop in our growth of practicing our faith, though in a sense we remain with the disposition of children in our relationship with God, loving and relying on our heavenly Father as children do with their loving parents.[76] Additionally, as

---

[76] Matt. 18:2–4: "I tell you truly that unless you change and become like little children, you shall not enter the kingdom of heaven. Therefore, whoever

already stated, we must not stop at the level of a child in our knowledge and understanding of the Catholic Faith.

Just as professional people continue to learn and study after they have completed their academic or professional studies and degrees, continuing to be updated and current in matters pertaining to their profession, so we must continue to grow in matters of faith so that we can use the talents the Lord has bestowed upon us responsibly. We are to be productive, as in the case of the two of the three men that managed well what was entrusted to them in the Parable of the Ten Talents.[77] Their lord rewarded them generously for showing responsibility with what he had entrusted to them.

Jimmy is now completing the last two years of elementary school and beginning middle school. On the human level, the young man is expected to be more responsible and accountable for his behavior, making choices with an increasing awareness of their consequences for better or worse. He is expected to be more discerning in choosing friends and which relationships and activities to either pursue, terminate, or avoid. His physiology also changes; adolescence awakens Jimmy's sexuality, and all kind of urges that were previously silent now begin to surface, sometimes taking complete control of his thoughts and behavior. This inner personal revolution within a young adolescent can be very powerful — and very confusing.

These are "difficult years" not only for Jimmy, but also for his parents, teachers, and friends. The childhood phase is over, has passed into the pages of personal history, and will never return. Jimmy's pattern of behavior begins to change at home, at school, and

---

humbles himself like this little child is the greatest in the kingdom of heaven." See also ibid. 19:14; Mark 10:15; Luke 18:17. St. Paul says in 1 Cor. 14:20: "Brothers and sisters, stop being irresponsible in your thinking. Be like infants in respect to evil, but in your thinking be mature."

77   Matt. 25:14–30.

outside of both places. He is not yet a fully mature adult, though he considers himself to be so and frequently feels misjudged and almost excluded by older adults. He has recurrent mood swings, and increasingly feels the need to assert himself, insisting on being recognized and counted. Whereas his physical growth is rapid, his emotional and intellectual levels grow at a slow pace.

As a young adult, Jimmy begins to look for comrades among his peer group. It is a time of great inner and outer conflict, with an insistence on self-reliance and seeking acceptance and approval of friends. Jimmy wants to be autonomous, yet at the same time tries his best to conform with his peers. He goes where the group goes, and adopts his comrades' behavior, language, jokes, and outfits. He spends hours texting or talking on his iPhone with others who are his age. If others in the group grow beards, so does he; if they adopt a certain hairstyle, so does he; if they do drugs, he might attempt to experiment; if they watch porn, he might consider doing so, too; if they complain bitterly about anything at home and school, so does he; if they sleep around, he might entertain this idea. If the youth, male and female, are today audacious and carefree, tomorrow they are taciturn, almost vexed. Jimmy is no exception to these challenges and peer pressures.

Girls, in this phase of development, are the first to develop an interested in boys (whom they perceive as being immature) and enter the phase of "boy crazy." Eventually boys get interested in girls as they enter their own stage of "girl crazy." They will feel mushy and romantic. At school Jimmy may fall in love a number of times, not knowing if the girl has noticed him, much less how she feels about him. At a certain point, Jimmy might find the need to open up to someone and try to decipher what is happening in his personal life.

While all of this is going on, Jimmy is studying and preparing himself to receive the Sacrament of Confirmation.[78] Ironically, while Jimmy might be having his personal crisis in relating to the Church, he is also preparing to become an authentic witness of the Lord and thereby responsible to spread the Faith through his lifestyle.

All of this might sound and feel very unsettling. But, in fact, this is one of those moments when Jimmy needs God more than ever, and this is why he will receive the sevenfold gifts of the Holy Spirit when he is confirmed. They are wisdom, understanding, counsel, fortitude, knowledge, piety, and fear of the Lord.[79] He will need to make use of them for the rest of his life and should not postpone their use until any tomorrow, for postponing till tomorrow might mean never — as one proverb states, the road to Hell is paved with good intentions. Furthermore, if he manages to hold on to Sunday Mass, he will be fine eventually. This connection with the Lord is essential for Jimmy so that he can speak to his loving and caring Redeemer, Who is fully present in Holy Eucharist.

✠ ✠ ✠

Very early in the Church, the anointing with the Oil of Sacred Chrism, consecrated by the bishop at the Chrism Mass, was added to the laying on of hands on the candidate during the Confirmation ceremony. It signifies that the young person being confirmed, as a baptized person, is anointed just as Christ had been anointed by the Holy Spirit.[80]

It should come as no surprise when an adolescent's issues also challenge adults to reflect on the issues in their personal, family, professional, and spiritual lives. Witnessing the Sacrament of Confirmation reminds all of us adults that we have received the Gifts

[78] See chap. 3.
[79] CCC 1831.
[80] Acts 10:38.

of the Holy Spirit and are called to put them into practice in our contemporary world, which can be full of upheaval, as well as in our personal lives, where inner peace may become elusive.

As adults, we must continually ask ourselves if our knowledge, understanding, and faith have kept pace with our intellectual and professional growth. Are our God-given talents being used for self or altruistic service? Are we providing assistance to the poor and marginalized? Are we self-regulating our intellectual and emotional responses in difficult and, at times, frustrating, confusing, and unsettling situations? Is our sexuality being celebrated as a gift from God or an expression of selfishness and hedonism? Are we being responsible and accountable to God, family, the Church, coworkers, subordinates, and also to ourselves? Are we setting a good example for the younger generation and encouraging youth to be heard and their contributions and insights welcomed — something that requires a lot of humility and patience?

As Jimmy prepares to commit himself to God and the Church through the Sacrament of Confirmation, he reminds adults that our spiritual life is not based on how far we can go without committing a serious sin, but how far we should go to become holy. The authentic Catholic is not one who wants to know how much he can get away with on the moral level, but rather how much he can contribute to make the world a better place by having a very close relationship with the Lord.

Finally, Jimmy, like most youth, tends to put faith in the back seat at this time of his life, rather than making it a priority. However, receiving the Sacrament of Confirmation should help him to stop and think about his value system and where he is heading. So, he challenges adults to live a better life of faith, leading and inspiring by example. As Pope Francis said during the homily in a Canonization Mass on

Sunday, October 9, 2002: "Faith invites us to acknowledge constantly that we are in need of healing and forgiveness, and to share in the frailty of those who are near to us, without feeling ourselves superior."[81]

As Jimmy finishes high school, he must decide whether to go on to college or find a full-time occupation. His parents should take part in this discernment. This choice should be made with great diligence and foresight because it will have lifelong implications. He needs to assess his gifts, his potential, his aptitude, and the current family and personal financial situation, because going to college is a very expensive enterprise.

It is hoped that Jimmy will settle down as he approaches his final year of high school. He might be tempted to goof off, to get caught up in something that is not important for adult life, to go with the crowd, to not be interested in thinking seriously about his future. In other words, Jimmy needs to dedicate personal time to discern. He will be wise if he carries out his discernment with input from his parents and those who want him to succeed.

Should Jimmy decide to go to college, he will do well to remember the words of Jordan Peterson: "Your life becomes meaningful in precise proportion to the depths of the responsibility you are willing to shoulder." Some young people think that college exists to give them a carefree lifestyle for four years, with their parents footing the piling bills. They experiment with their lives, indulge in drinking and drugs, and engage in other forms of irresponsible and risky behavior. For a time, they may act as though they are invincible, attending games on the weekends, partying, neglecting their studies, and engaging in activities that really can derail the course they have set for themselves.

---

[81] Francis, Homily at the Canonization Mass of Saints Giovanni Battista Scalabrini and Artemede Zatti (October 9, 2022).

Jimmy has to be on the alert not to be lured into such self-defeating behavior. He is in dire need of God and sound guidance. He needs to make good choices and foster healthy friendships. He must fulfill his duty as a student, study hard, and make sure he relaxes rather than being completely absorbed by study to the detriment of his physical, emotional, mental, and spiritual health and growth. He needs to be in contact with God not only by daily prayer, but sacramentally, especially in Holy Mass and the Sacrament of Penance and Reconciliation. He needs to give back to the community as a dedicated Catholic, performing corporal works of mercy. Of course, he should be involved in academic clubs, but he must also attend to those in need. Some confreres might think that he is an oddball. In fact, he is a sound and thoughtful young man. In other words, he is getting his priorities straight.

A Rainbow Moment

God wants Jimmy to succeed—just as He wants the best for each of us. The prophet Jeremiah declared many centuries ago: "I know the plans I have in mind for you, plans for your welfare and not for misfortune, plans that will give you a future full of hope."[82] Like Jimmy, we must utilize the gift of wisdom, which we received at Confirmation. If you know someone like Jimmy, take a moment to pray now, that God would help him make wise Christian choices—and, if he veers off course, that God will send a sign of his love, to help him get back on track ... something amazing on his way to Heaven.

[82] Jer. 29:11.

CHAPTER EIGHT

Intimacy Issues

JIMMY THINKS GOD HAS called him to married life, rather than the priesthood or religious life. He has begun dating and is learning how to deal with his personal sexuality, recognizing that it is a gift from God that can be easily misused and abused. And he recognizes that the sexual union between one husband and his one wife within the context of a sacramental Marriage is sacred, whether they are Catholic or not.

In the coming years, Jimmy will face many challenges and temptations in this area of his life. Most likely he will fall in and out of love a number of times in his young life, each breakup potentially leaving an emotional scar that needs to be healed. But because our society tends to idolize anything sex-related, including pornography, the widespread attitude that separates sexual intimacy from marriage has not only led to immoral and irresponsible sexual encounters but also to the abuse and dehumanization of the other person. Tragically, few take the time to consider the moral aspects of what they are doing, beyond what secular law requires of them.

✠   ✠   ✠

In 2012, Pope Benedict XVI was speaking with a group of bishops from the Midwestern United States when he identified the twofold challenge facing marriage and family life: the low appreciation of the unbreakable marriage covenant and the rejection, even among Catholics, of a "responsible, mature sexual ethic grounded in the practice of chastity."[83] He challenged the bishops to teach the youth an authentic Catholic vision of sexuality and love. Of course, such an education cannot take place or be taken seriously if parents, educators, and even religious leaders themselves do not grasp the holiness of sexuality.

Pope Blessed John Paul I once recounted this story to illustrate the importance of the Church in the life of a young person:

> There was once … a street preacher at the Speaker's Corner in Hyde Park, London. A disheveled man kept heckling him. At one point, the man yelled, "The Church has been around for two thousand years. Yet, the world is still full of thieves, adulterers and murderers." The preacher was very quick in his reply: "Sir, you are absolutely right. However, water has been around for two million years and just look at the state of your dirty neck."

> It is a fact that there have been bad popes, bad priests, and bad Catholics. But does this mean that the Gospels have been followed? Absolutely not! Rather, it is the opposite. In those cases, the Gospel message was not applied.[84]

Sexual temptations have always been found throughout human history because human nature remains the same. The Lord's call for personal chastity remains a perennial invitation and challenge, even to married couples.

---

[83] Benedict XVI, Address to the Bishops of the United States of America from Region VIII during Their "Ad Limina Apostolorum" (March 9, 2012).

[84] *Letters Written by Blessed John Paul I — as Cardinal-Patriarch Albino Luciani*, trans. Msgr. Laurence J. Spiteri (2022), pp. 72–73.

✠   ✠   ✠

Jimmy is learning that loving and personal feelings are very complicated matters. He has to learn to make personal sacrifices, exercise self-control, keep away from bad company, resist peer pressure, and avoid talk and programs that are near occasions of sin. He might be tempted to live with his girlfriend and feel very constrained by the Catholic moral code. However, if he were to look at when he acquired his license to drive a car, he should quickly discover something parallel.

Society has rightly set specific rules for driving so as to protect both drivers and passengers. There are traffic police, traffic lights, yellow lines, one-way streets, no-parking zones, and so forth. Before he receives a driver's license, a prospective driver's knowledge of the rules is examined, and he is given a driving test. The driver must abide by these rules, both for his own sake and that of others.

Just as we place limits and restrictions on drivers for the good of all, so must we observe God's design of human sexuality, and abide by principles of sexual morality. On the moral level, Jimmy has to abide by Christian sexual mores; he must respect his girlfriend, show affection in an honorable and proper way, and control his own impulses. Above all, he must pursue the virtue of chastity.

Everyone, whether single or married, is called to live the virtue of chastity according to his or her state of life. This calls for a very delicate, difficult, and complicated balance to keep, because our society bombards us with all kinds of sexual messages, images, and allurements.

Jimmy's struggles with sexuality give those in his life opportunity to stop and evaluate their own sexual attitudes, relationships, and behavior. Jimmy's struggle to live a chaste life should inspire others to do the same. And whenever Jimmy fails in this area, he can seek God's forgiveness in the Sacrament of Penance and

Reconciliation, and be comforted that God is always very merciful, loving, patient, and forgiving of human frailty.

Our society tells us that if we are not sexually active, there is something wrong with us. In fact, it is society that has got it all wrong. Each of us is free and independent, responsible for our personal decisions and actions. We do not have to follow the crowd, though we must always consider the "call to love," and how our actions help or harm others.

Jimmy will come to understand that there are many ways of expressing his love, caring and supporting his girlfriend without any genital sexual activity. God created the natural desire for a man and a woman to be physically (sexually) united, yet this desire is intended to be ordered toward a unity that is exclusive, permanent, and open to new life (children).

The biblical message is very clear: God intended sexual desire to draw people of opposite sexes to marriage and not simply to sexual activity. It teaches that marriage is part of God's plan, permanent, exclusive, open to new life, and a sacred covenant that reflects the union between Christ and His Church.[85]

The purpose of Jimmy's dating is not only to discover who the other person is, but also to learn more about himself. This is why Jimmy should pray to the Holy Spirit to guide and illuminate him in finding and choosing the right future spouse. Jimmy and his girlfriend should discern together whether they should go on with their relationship or break it off and seek another person. They should seek and listen to the advice of the wise and not intrusive busybodies.

Jimmy will learn a lot about himself by the way he treats his girlfriend. He will discover if they have the same values in common and

---

[85] These are some of the many references: Matt. 5:28; 19:4–9; Mark 10:6–12; Luke 16:18; Eph. 4:19; 5:3, 25–28, 33; Col. 3:5; 1 Cor. 6:13, 18–19; 7:2–5; 2 Cor. 11:2; 1 Thess. 4:3–7; Gal. 5:16–21; Rom. 1:24; 7:3.

the same dreams about a future life together, and he will discern when it is time for them to get engaged to be married. They should discover their strong and weak points. They should learn how to support one another on many levels and help each other grow in their strong points and confront, learn, and work on their weak points. This happens properly only if Jimmy and his girlfriend pray together, discern together, and grow together. In other words, it is done through constructive communication on the human and spiritual levels.

Jimmy and his girlfriend Jenny discern that they are meant for one another, and commit to helping one another — and eventually their whole family — get to Heaven. They promise to offer mutual lifelong support as they deepen their friendship with the Lord and one another. Of course, this does not happen instantaneously, but slowly over time.

Finally, a very nervous Jimmy proposes, and Jenny gladly accepts. Their feelings are beyond description. Family and friends are very happy for them and look forward to the wedding day. Jimmy and Jenny ask their family priest, Fr. Nate, to have a religious betrothal ceremony (Rite of Betrothal) wherein the engagement rings are blessed and exchanged. The wedding date is set and marriage preparations begin in earnest. The engaged couple stand as a reminder to other engaged couples and married persons to look back at what prompted them to seek marriage, to recall the nervousness and joy of the moment of proposing, to reminisce about how they have progressed in achieving their common dreams and goals, to celebrate their mutual love, and to thank the Lord for His many blessings through their loving relationship.

A Rainbow Moment

Single adults need to carefully evaluate their interpersonal relationships and see what is wanting and what should be kept; what they should strengthen, and how to diminish weaknesses. Love and loving are very risky because we might be rejected and abandoned if we are completely honest with another person. This is why prayer is so important.

It is important to watch for signs that a relationship has run its course, or that God is taking the other person in a different direction. For example, if there is a lack of trust—if one partner is unable to share things about himself for fear of being rejected or discarded—this is a sure sign that it is not a healthy relationship and lacks honest communication.

What happens in dating is a preview of what will happen during marriage. It is normal to have struggles, private concerns, disagreements, and spats. These present opportunities to learn, forgive, be patient, and grow from such experiences. This is only possible if both partners are able to say, "I am truly sorry" and understand the importance of forgiving.[86] If they are able to do that, something amazing happens on our way to Heaven, thanks to Jimmy and Jenny's love story. It is an inspiring rainbow.

[86]   Francis, General Audience (May 13, 2015).

CHAPTER NINE

The Gift of Marital Love

JIMMY AND JENNY'S BIG day is almost here: their wedding day. Wedding preparations have been intense, somewhat hectic, and very time-consuming. There were some tense budget negotiations on the wedding reception venue, the selection of the menu, and their honeymoon destination. They even unsuccessfully tried to bargain with the photographer.

Jimmy and Jenny have paid attention to details. The readings and prayers for the wedding Mass have been chosen; the readers have been selected; the wedding dress and bridesmaids' dresses have been purchased and altered. They have decided who will take whom to the rehearsal and then to the church on the day of the wedding, and who will be seated where on both occasions. All these decisions — from the spiritual to the mundane — are behind them.

Their wedding day dawns, bright and clear and perfect; the projected rain never materializes. As she dresses, Jenny thinks of the words of St. Paul, when he reminds the Corinthians that marriage is a gift from the Lord.[87]

Dressed in their wedding finery, the bridal party — from the best man and maid of honor to the little flower girl and ring bearer — are ready to participate in the wedding ceremony. The

---

[87] 1 Cor. 7:7.

wedding is scheduled to take place at Jenny's parish church, with Fr. Nate, their favorite priest, presiding. The couple have studied Natural Family Planning to prepare them for parenthood.

✠   ✠   ✠

All of these wedding day preparations invite us to recall our own Catholic vocation — and anticipate our wedding day with the Lord at the end of our lives. One day, the first Maltese saint, St. George Preca (1880–1962), was giving a retreat to some religious sisters. He asked for a show of hands of those who wanted to die. No hand went up. He then asked them if they were willing to wed the Lord because, as long as they remain on earth, they are only engaged to Him.[88]

What we do or fail to do during the course of our lives is part of our preparation for going to Heaven. It is said that life is not a rehearsal; it is the real thing. The readings and the prayers for our heavenly marriage will consist of the spiritual readings that enrich our thoughts, and of the prayers of praise and thanksgiving to God we offer during our lifetime. Our "readers," those who proclaim and teach the Lord's message, are already selected by Divine Providence. They are those who lead, govern, minister, and serve the members of the Church. Our wedding dress was given to us at our Baptism; our bridal party consists of the members of the Church, especially our parish community, and particularly our family, which the Second Vatican Council refers to as the domestic church.[89]

On our own heavenly "wedding day," our maid of honor and best man shall be Our Lady and St. Joseph, and the congregation shall consist of the community of saints and the angels. Our home parish is Heaven, and the presiding priest is Jesus Christ the Eternal High

---

[88] Ġorġ Borg, *San Ġorġ Preca, Ħaj Bħal Qatt Qabel* (Preca, 2021).
[89] *Lumen gentium*, no. 11. See also *CCC* 2685.

Priest. Our spiritual journey prepares us for our heavenly wedding by being a life of growing in holiness, though at times it is hectic; we may fail in patience and trust, or violate the tenets of love of God and neighbor, yet we can always seek forgiveness from our Groom.

Our heavenly banquet will be more beautiful than words can express. The menu is Holy Eucharist. The flowers on our spiritual crown shall be the virtues we live out on earth with the Lord's help. As we reflect upon Jimmy and Jenny's wedding, let us also consider heavenly life and how we are preparing for our own heavenly wedding.

✠   ✠   ✠

Where will Jimmy and Jenny celebrate their very special wedding? They could marry at city hall or in front of a judge. They could marry in a hotel or on the beach or by a swimming pool or in their parents' home or backyard. They might have chosen to go to Las Vegas or Atlantic City and marry in one of the quaint wedding chapels. However, they are committed Catholics, and so they choose to marry in a Catholic church. In so doing, they decide to enter into a sacramental Marriage, wherein Christ shall remain silently present throughout their married life.[90]

Why is entering into a sacramental Marriage in the Church important? Because Catholic Marriage is a sacrament, the Lord bestows upon these unions special graces, giving spouses the ability to live out their mutual love, which should imbue every corner of their respective lives with the virtues of faith, hope, and charity as they journey toward Heaven as individuals and as a couple. A Catholic wedding ceremony invites everyone present to recall that marriage is

---

90   Francis, *Letter to Married Couples for the "Amoris Laetitia Family" Year, 2021–2022* (December 26, 2021).

a holy lifestyle and vocation for, as St. Paul teaches, "everything which God has created in good."[91]

During the wedding ceremony, Jimmy is asked to state his intentions in marrying Jenny. He is asked if he is truly free, willing, and prepared to marry Jenny; he is asked if he is ready to enter lifelong marriage with Jenny (indissolubility), if he is willing to be exclusively faithful to Jenny for his entire married life (fidelity), and if he will accept children and bring them up as Catholics (openness to life). Jenny is asked the same questions. After the couple give their positive individual responses to each of the three questions, the presiding priest seeks the individual marital consent of both parties through the exchange of the Marriage vows. The priest ends by saying: "May the Lord in His kindness strengthen the consent you have declared before the Church and graciously bring to fulfillment His blessings within you. What God has joined, let no one put asunder." This is followed by the exchange of the blessed wedding rings.

Finally, the groom and bride are declared "man and wife" and presented to the assembled community. Some tears are shed, noses are blown, beaming smiles appear. There is great joy in the air. Married life has begun its adventurous journey as the Sacrament of Marriage is lived every day of their life together until death. In essence, marital love is not about feelings, though these help abundantly, but about a lifelong commitment.

Jimmy and Jenny should remember to put each other first, and God above all, in their marriage. When problems invariably arise, they must not run to their respective parents, other family members, or friends to resolve some issue without first sitting down together,

---

[91] 1 Tim. 4:4. This includes the fact that the sexual relationship between the couple is a divine gift and cannot be used as a weapon or as a reward or punishment by either spouse. St. Paul exhorts the Corinthians: "Do not refuse one another" (1 Cor. 7:5).

communicating honestly with each other, and working hard together to resolve the issue. They should recall what God declared in the Book of Genesis: "Therefore a man shall leave his father and mother and cleave to his wife, and they shall become one flesh."[92]

✠   ✠   ✠

If you are married, what do you recall of your own wedding ceremony? When a couple expresses their intentions to live the Sacrament of Marriage, they declare that they freely, willingly, and faithfully commit to each other for the rest of their lives. Furthermore, they promise to be open to physically becoming parents. For some couples, this may entail being open to receiving, willingly and with gratitude, any children God might entrust to their care.

What does it mean to be "faithful" in marriage? Exclusive fidelity involves not just sexual fidelity but emotional fidelity as well.[93] Marital conflicts often arise over one spouse being "married" (giving the highest priority to) his or her blood family or friends or career or hobbies. These put at risk the marital bond. For example, some couples with interfering family members need to set boundaries during the engagement period. If these family members persist in interfering after the wedding, the couple must make their union a priority. Each of their families will play a very important role in their married life and subsequently in the lives of the children born of this union. However, families are there to help and not to run the show, so to speak.

Parents with married children must ask themselves if they are interfering with the children's married life and, if so, to search for the means to stop. Undue influence can ruin even the best of marriages

<hr>

[92]   Gen. 2:24.
[93]   See Gen. 2:24.

because it can sow great tension, discord, and hard feelings. Thus, intrusive parents, relatives, and friends are challenged to realize what harm they might be doing, despite good intentions.

The three daughters of the famous movie giants, Paul Newman and his wife Joanne Woodward, described their parents' marriage as one with many crises, but also the parents' determination to remain married to one another — something they did for fifty years.[94] A couple must work together, struggle together, and be mutually determined to go beyond problems that are facing them. Keep in mind that Jesus is present in a sacramental Marriage, and couples should call on Him every day and ask Him to provide them with more special graces attached to this Sacrament.

[94] The posthumous memoirs of the actor in *The Extraordinary Life of an Ordinary Man* (Knopf, 2022).

A Rainbow Moment

Weddings are a timely invitation to married couples to reflect on their own value system and how this is affecting their marriage. Have they given priority to their marital commitment? Have they been open to life from the physical union of their bodies? Have they done their best to show spiritual, emotional, and economic support to one another? Are there areas where personal improvement is required, either as a spouse or as a parent?

Pope Francis once observed, "Love is demanding, yes, but it is beautiful, and the more we allow ourselves to be involved by it, the more we discover true happiness in it. And now, let each one of us ask themselves: How is my love? Is it faithful? Is it generous? Is it creative? How are our families? Are they open to life, to the gift of children?"[95]

Do you have a sacramental Marriage? If not, consider how you might resolve this situation with the assistance of a priest or a deacon. If for some reason there is an impediment that cannot be resolved, talk with a priest about how the provisions enacted by Pope Francis in *Amoris laetitia* might apply to it.[96] In any case, consider how you

---

[95]   Francis, Angelus, (October 6, 2024).

[96]   Chapter 8 of Pope Francis's post-synodal apostolic exhortation *Amoris laetitia* (March 19, 2016) heartens, "a responsible personal and pastoral discernment of particular cases, one which would recognize that, since 'the degree of responsibility is not equal in all cases', the consequences or effects

are carrying out your family obligations to one
another and to your children. Has your commitment
remained free, faithful, total, and life-giving? Is it oriented
toward your mutual sanctification? Throughout their lives,
and through their vocation, each married couple is called
back to God or to deepen their relationship with God. This
is another one of God's rainbows, something amazing that
happens on our way to Heaven.

of a rule need not necessarily always be the same" (no. 300), and the Pope
goes on to write, "I would also point out that the Eucharist 'is not a prize
for the perfect, but a powerful medicine and nourishment for the weak'"
(n. 351).

CHAPTER TEN

Establishing a Home

THE WEDDING DAY AND the honeymoon have passed into history. Now Jimmy and Jenny return to the adventures, challenges, vicissitudes, and blessings of daily married life.

Jimmy and Jenny decided before getting married that Jimmy would work outside the house, whereas Jenny would work at home. One of the great injustices in our society is that we think of work in terms of a paycheck and prestige. Stay-at-home wives and mothers work very hard, although they don't get paid for their work — and many among us are conditioned to think that the bigger the paycheck, the greater one's importance. If married men would stay home for a month and do the work that their wives do, they would doubtless be very surprised by how hard it is to be a wife and mother at home. It is essential that husbands and wives work together to encourage and support one another, as best they can, to fulfill their respective roles and responsibilities at home.

Marriage and parenthood are God-given vocations. These vocations, like any other vocation, are concrete commitments that require deep dedication, very hard work, perseverance, and generous self-giving. A vocation is not an eight-to-five job. Indeed, it requires twenty-four hours' commitment, seven days a week. In a way, this great dedication is putting into action what the Lord said: "No one has greater love than this, that someone would lay down his life for his friends."[97] This constant outpouring of altruistic love and caring can neither go forward nor make sense without divine assistance (grace). God is ever ready to grant it when He is simply called upon. Our Lady, who was a wife and a mother, will intercede in every wife's and mother's humble request: "Help me!"

One of the hardest aspects of parenting is the silent self-blame that occurs when one of the children — especially an adult child — makes choices not in keeping with how they were raised. Parents often blame themselves for the resulting misfortune and heartbreak. But we must remember that the adult child is responsible for personal decisions and behavior. Family life is very complex and presents many challenges. Parents have to let go of their child once the age of majority has been reached. Their parenting now is to pray, and to provide support and sound advice to help their adult child work toward independence.

✠   ✠   ✠

The Apostolic Exhortation *Amoris laetitia* opens with these wonderful words: "The joy of love experienced by families is also the joy of the Church."[98] This papal declaration is of extreme importance because it directly links the married couple and their family with the Church, the greater household of God.[99] In a limited way, this declaration is stating that the existential status of the Church is linked directly to the existential status of those who are married and their respective families.

In first-world countries, and especially in the United States, the character and expectations of marriage have greatly changed for the worse over the last sixty years. Today, only about half of adult

---

[97] John 15:13.

[98] Francis, *Amoris laetitia*, no. 1.

[99] 1 Tim. 3:15: "members of God's household, the church of the living God."

Americans are married.[100] This percentage is down from the 72 percent of married couples in 1960. The average age of marriage today is around thirty years of age. There has been a slow, subtle, and steady decline rate of people getting married. Many young adults seem to perceive marriage as obsolete and are opting to co-habit rather than marry. In so doing, they fail to consider the core values that sustain marriage, and how important those values are to intimate relationships.

Dr. William Bradford Wilcox, the director of the National Marriage Project and professor of sociology at the University of Virginia, wrote that "marriage conveys a sense of meaning, purpose, direction and stability that tends to benefit adults and especially children. People who get married have an expectation of sexual fidelity, and that fidelity tends to engender a sense of trust and security ... There is no kind of similar solemn ritual marking the beginning of cohabitation."[101]

So why are couples choosing to cohabit? One prevalent excuse young people offer most often is because "everyone else does it." And yet people who cohabit without the benefit of marriage are cheating themselves of the graces they need to carry out the lifetime commitment that marriage represents — including facing hardships, challenges, and other serious troubles between themselves and within their families. Cohabitation is a bit like driving a car with your eyes on your phone — the immediate distractions prevent you from anticipating and safely navigating the dangers ahead!

[100] D'Vera Cohn et al. "Barely Half of U.S. Adults Are Married — A Record Low," Pew Research, December 14, 2011, https://www.pewresearch.org/social-trends/2011/12/14/barely-half-of-u-s-adults-are-married-a-record-low/.

[101] Aja Gabel, "The Marriage Crisis: How Marriage Has Changed in the Last 50 Years and Why It Continues to Decline," *Virginia*, summer 2012.

Living out a sacramental Marriage is important not only for the well-being of society at large, but for providing meaning, purpose, direction, and stability to the married couple and to their children. It elevates a couple's intentions to share their lives together into a vocation and a holy lifestyle. What is more, secular governments have traditionally supported and subtly promoted marriage because it serves as the bedrock of society.

Many joys and sorrows, personal successes and failures, tears of joy and of sorrow, intimate conversations and comfortable silences, and understandings and misunderstandings are part and parcel of married life; no one escapes them. And yet, when a couple vows to stay married in good times and in bad, in sickness and in health, "until death parts us," they cannot just give up when experiencing unsettling situations. They should always keep in mind that they are never abandoned by the silent Jesus, Who is always present in their union. As St. George Preca once told a newlywed couple, paint in huge letters on the walls of every room of your home: "Practice patience." Marital life requires the patient, intentional practice of all the virtues St. Paul lists in his letter to the Church at Corinth, which is read at many weddings:

> Love is patient and kind. Love does not envy nor boasts. Love is not arrogant or rude. Love does not insist on its own way, is not self-seeking, is not easily angered or irritable or resentful, and keeps no record of wrongs. Love is not self-satisfied in evil but rejoices with the truth. Love bears all things, believes all things, hopes all things, perseveres in all things. (1 Cor. 13:4–7)

The Sacrament of Marriage does not finish with the exchange of marital vows but is a lifelong celebration. Therefore, the couple should let Jesus inside their personal lives, their marriage, and their home, and allow Him to always assist them by remaining in their midst. After all, the covenant of marriage is a reflection of the union between Christ and His Church.[102]

Pope Francis said,

> We can say that whenever a man and a woman fall in love, God offers them a gift; that gift is marriage. It is a marvelous gift, which contains the power of God's own love: strong, enduring, faithful, ready to start over after every failure or moment of weakness. Marriage is not a formality you go through. You don't get married in order to be 'card-carrying' Catholics, to obey a rule, or because the Church tells you to, or to have a party … No, you get married *because you want to build your marriage on the love of Christ,* which is solid as rock. In marriage, Christ gives himself to you, so that you can find the strength to give yourselves to one another. So take heart: family life is not "mission impossible"! By the grace of the sacrament, God makes it a wonderful journey, to be undertaken together with him and never alone. The family is not a lofty ideal that is unattainable in reality. God solemnly promises his presence in your marriage and family, not only on the day of your wedding, but for the rest of your lives. And he keeps supporting you, every day of your journey.[103]

✠　✠　✠

Children are an important part of God's plan for marriage and family life. At their wedding ceremony, Jimmy and Jenny profess their

---

[102] Eph. 5:31–32.

[103] Francis, Address at X World Meeting of Families: Festival of Families (June 22, 2022), no. 1.

openness to new life, to children. In doing so, they affirm their desire to participate not only in the continuity of their proper family, but of the Church and human society at large.

When married couples have and raise their children, they are mirroring and sharing in God's creative work. It is true that having and raising children can be very challenging and very expensive, and yet when a couple is generous with God, He always provides what is needed — and teaches a couple, through their children, to live simply, prudently, and prayerfully. Above all, they learn that the greatest gift they can give a child is love.

Married couples with children must rely on the graces God gives them on their wedding day to face the family problems that may come — sometimes very serious ones. From the very beginning, Sacred Scripture speaks of the pain, evil, and violence that can break up families. Even the first family experienced this, when Adam and Eve's son Cain murdered his brother Abel.[104] As the Book of Genesis unfolds, there are terrible conflicts between the respective sons and wives of Abraham, Isaac, and Jacob. Out of jealousy, Jacob's sons went so far as to sell their brother Joseph into slavery.[105]

Even those who love and follow God experience great tragedies. Think of King David's sons, one of whom even rebelled against David and sought his life.[106] And even the great King David had great flaws that had tragic effects: his adulterous affair with Bathsheba induced David to murder his lover's husband.[107] Marital issues and problems have always been around.

One of the most common areas of contention for married couples is money — and the expense of raising children is often cited as the

---

[104] Gen. 4:1–10.
[105] Gen. 37:18–36.
[106] 2 Sam. 15:1–31; 18:1–19:15.
[107] 2 Sam. 11:1–27.

reason for limiting family size. However, children are unique blessings from God Himself.[108] He did not create Adam and Eve and tell them to just remain by themselves. Rather, God directed the first couple to be fruitful and increase; in other words, to share their lives with their children. [109] Sacred Scripture speaks about children being a gift from God — an understanding that existed in civil society up to recent times.

Pope St. John Paul II spoke about this in a homily at Puebla de los Ángeles, Mexico: "Our God in his deepest mystery is not a solitude, but a family, for he has within himself fatherhood, sonship and the essence of the family, which is love." That love, in the divine family, is the Holy Spirit. The family is thus not unrelated to God's very being.[110]

There is currently a trend in which men and women remain proudly "child free," as if having children is some kind of imprisonment. Pope Francis has spoken against this on at least two occasions. During one general audience, he stated: "Many couples do not have children because they do not want to, or they have just one because they do not want any more, but they have two dogs, two cats.... Yes, dogs and cats take the place of children.... And this denial of fatherhood or motherhood diminishes us, it takes away our humanity.... A man or a woman who [does] not voluntarily develop a sense of fatherhood or motherhood [is] lacking something fundamental, something important."[111]

Again, on September 4, 2024, Pope Francis reiterated this message while addressing the President of Indonesia and the Diplomatic Corps: "With a law of death, that is by limiting births, limiting the greatest richness that a nation can have, its births. Your country, meanwhile, has families with three, four, and five children.... Keep

---

[108] For example, Gen. 22:17; 48:4; Deut. 7:13; 28:4; Ps. 127:3.

[109] Gen. 2:28; 9:7.

[110] John Paul II, Homily, Puebla de los Ángeles (January 28, 1979).

[111] Francis, General Audience (January 5, 2022).

going like this. It is an example for all countries. It may seem funny that perhaps some families prefer to have a cat or a small dog, and not a child, but this is not right."[112]

Overpopulation or concerns about pollution are often cited as reasons couples ought to limit the number of children they have or to opt not to have any children of their own. In reality, the birth rate of many Western countries has led to population decline.[113] And by giving in to this false social narrative, couples are denying themselves the blessings of an active family life: growing deeper in love, much joy, comfort, blessings, a deeper understanding of themselves and their marital relationship, more caring, a better appreciation of their positive contribution to the Church and to society at large, and being able to discern better what really matters. The real challenge is finding ways to share our resources and the gifts of the earth rather than hoarding them. Together, we must all care for the world God has given us. And we must care for one another as we journey together toward Heaven.

---

[112] Francis, Address, Istana Negara Presidential Palace Hall (Jakarta, Indonesia)(September 4, 2024).

[113] "Birth Rate by Country 2025," World Population Review, accessed August 4, 2025, https://worldpopulationreview.com/country-rankings/birth-rate-by-country.

A Rainbow Moment

Have concerns about money or other resources been a factor in how you and your spouse have chosen to live out your marriage commitment or sustain your family? The vast majority of people are not born into money and do not inherit a fortune. They have to work very hard to earn a living.

Any kind of positive work contributes to the nourishment, stability, and prosperity of a person's family, and, in turn, of society. St. Paul insisted on the necessity of work, telling the Christians in Thessalonica, "For when we were with you, we had commanded you this, that no one who is unwilling to work shall eat."[114] Many do not think or realize that work is an essential part of human dignity.[115]

Young, hardworking parents such as Jimmy and Jenny invite all parents to reflect on the beauty of parenthood; on their collaboration with God; on asking themselves if they are truly love-giving to their children (rather than merely gift-giving), and whether they have truly entrusted their adult children to God. They remind us to ask ourselves whether we have called upon God and Our Lady to help us in our noble vocation. They cause us to ponder what God is asking of us with respect to working inside or outside the

---

[114] 2 Thess. 3:10.

[115] Francis, Regina Caeli Address (May 1, 2022).

home, according to the needs of our families.
They remind us to accept our respective limitations,
and to consider how much God is alive within the family
unit. Thus, we receive another one of God's rainbows,
something amazing that happens on our way to Heaven.

CHAPTER ELEVEN

Overcoming Obstacles

ONE OF THE GREATEST challenges that Jimmy and Jenny will have as a married couple and parents is creeping individualism and, in consequence, incremental isolation. This happens when the two "I"s do not become one "We" — when either one or both spouses hold on to complete independence and autonomy from the beginning, or when over time it begins to replace family accountability and responsibilities.

When this happens, unless the couple resolves to end this very tragic process, the marriage embarks on a slow, disillusioned, and painful death. Hence, the permanent character of the marital relationship is weakened and endangered. Mutual respect and dignity begin to flounder. The marital covenant becomes a burden rather than a blessing. The couple's spiritual life, which is aimed at sanctifying not only one another and their children, but also the entire human race because it is the vocation by which to travel the way to heaven, begins to evaporate. The spouses' guard against any threat to the marital vocation is let down. Serious trouble is just around the corner, and the high waves of secularism and today's narcissistic society, in deep love with individualism, begin to buffet against their family, slowly chipping it away.

The pledge that the spouses gave each other on their wedding day is buried in the past. Happy memories are forgotten. Honest communication, mutual support, and esteem begin to fade, and love begins to dim. Irritation, harsh words, ongoing criticism, resentment, anger, and frustration creep into daily conversation. Isolation increases, the silent treatment becomes more common, and even intimate marital relations can be weaponized and converted into a source of reward or punishment. Friends replace family instead of friends enriching family. The virtues of forgiveness, patience, accepting limitations, kindness, respect, mercy, and affirmation are practiced less and less often.

Finally, over time, the Lord becomes a stranger as the spouses become absorbed in their respective selves and more and more individualistic. Spouses and their children become disposable, easily thrown away in pursuit of an ever-eluding sense of personal fulfillment. Jimmy and Jenny will be confronted with such temptations, pressures, and challenges, but they must resist such things as individuals and as a united couple and perceive them as enemies to their vocation.

✠　✠　✠

One fine day, a blissful Jenny informs Jimmy that they are going to be parents. He is overwhelmed with joy. They discover that their conceived child is a boy. So they choose the name of Johnny for their baby. In time, they will generate three more children by following Natural Family Planning (NFP).

Parenting requires great dedication. Remember, the Lord Jesus Himself was born into a family, and He eventually restored marriage to an unbreakable bond and sacrament,[116] and the family to an earthly image of the Trinity.[117] "May Nazareth teach us what family life is, its communion of love, its austere and simple beauty, and its sacred and inviolable character."[118]

---

[116] Matt. 19:3–10; Mark 10:11–12; Luke 16:18.
[117] CCC 2205.
[118] CCC 533.

As Jenny's pregnancy progresses, with all of its ups and downs, worries and delights, the young couple have not only to support one another with loving words and gestures, but also to find time to be with each other. They must regularly go out on "dates," though they are now married. Jimmy accompanies Jenny when she goes to the obstetrician. He learns to be patient and supportive when she has morning sickness and/or does not feel well. In other words, they must do this as a united couple.

There are cries of joy and exhilaration when Johnny is born. The baby is shown off to family and friends. Soon, mother and child are home. Johnny is not yet placed in the beautiful room they prepared for him; he stays within the sight and earshot of his doting parents. He is never alone, even when sleeping. But, of course, now the dynamics between the new parents change due to the arrival of the little bundle of joy. They must discover how to meet Johnny's needs and continue to grow together in their marriage.

Parenting together is part of this growth. Parenting is a joint adventure and an ongoing experiment with each child. As parents can inform us from firsthand experience, it is a journey full of surprises.

Newborns require constant attention and care — and it is an exhausting undertaking. There are many sleepless nights, with an endless parade of diapers and clothing, baths and feeding, and anxious trips to the pediatrician when the baby shows the minutest signs of being uncomfortable or sick. Johnny's parents learn to distinguish between cries of hunger, gas, tiredness, or discomfort.

Jenny is Johnny's mother twenty-four seven at home, and Jimmy helps her when he is home from work. They also know that they cannot afford to ignore their own relationship, so they ask a family member or a babysitter to look after their child on occasion so they can spend time alone together. They also make it a priority to sit down and eat as a family, without the distraction of television or iPhone.

Jimmy and Jenny agree to approach their growing child with a united front and not risk giving their son conflicting messages about his behavior as he gets a little older. Johnny, in due time, will be taught about his personal hygiene and learn how to shower or bathe himself. (When he gets a little older, these daily practices will also be applied to his spiritual life, as Johnny learns to pray and prepare for the sacraments, to keep his soul fresh and clean.)

When Johnny begins to go to school, his parents help him learn how to read and write; help him with his homework; listen attentively to him, especially when he wishes to share something that has happened at school; and make time to play with their Johnny. Jenny's and Jimmy's tired bodies are recharged most of the time because there is joy. Most importantly, they learn to worship and pray together.

Finding time to do these things is not always easy. Parents need to sit down and evaluate their priorities and commitments and decide as a team their schedule as spouses and parents. Honest and constructive mutual communication and with God are essential. Deepening their faith and trust in the Lord and Our Lady, who was present as a parent at the wedding feast of Cana and supervised the growth of her Son, is part of the course.[119]

Jimmy and Jenny frequently recall that what they are doing is fulfilling their God-given vocation as spouses and parents, which not only enriches their lives, but also the Church and society at large. It is a very noble and worthwhile endeavor that requires hard work. Because of this, God must play a major role in their personal lives and remain an essential part of their marriage and family.

Raising children can be an exhausting undertaking. A baby cries at all hours of the night and day, and tending to all his little needs — from feeding and changing to consoling him when he is teething or awakens

---

[119] John 2:1–12.

from a bad dream — can be stressful. Coming home from a tough day of working outside or inside the home and transitioning to home life can be hard work, too. Yet hard work has its payoffs: the Lord consoles us with happy moments together, with a sense of connectedness and contribution to family, Church, and society. Jimmy feels a growing sense of pride when he gets compliments about little Johnny (though, like any child, Johnny has his moments and even embarrasses his parents in public at times). Jenny feels renewed each time she looks at Johnny's innocent face, which radiates love; his hugs and kisses; his first steps and words, especially "I love you." Each night as they tuck in their little boy, Johnny's parents hold his little hands and thank the Lord for making them a family.

In this way, Jimmy and Jenny are imitating the loving care and protection of God regarding His children. Jimmy and Jenny should expand their vision to go beyond the fruit of their love and see that the little person in their home is living hope for tomorrow's world and defying those members in our society who are cynical and dismissive of children. Jimmy and Jenny, as devoted spouses and good parents, send an important message to society that family is indispensable for society and must be protected by civil law.

St. Paul, writing to the Christians of Corinth, spoke about this essential witness, which also applies to parents: "We are God's co-workers; you are God's field, God's building. According to the grace of God given to me, like a wise master builder I laid a foundation, and another is building upon it. But each one must be careful how he builds upon it, for no one can lay a foundation other than the one that is there, namely, Jesus Christ."[120] In *Amoris laetitia*, Pope Francis writes: "I thank God that many families, which are far from

---

[120] 1 Cor. 3:9–11.

considering themselves perfect, live in love, fulfil their calling and keep moving forward, even if they fall many times along the way."[121]

The Christian lifestyle is cradled and rooted in the family. Jimmy and Jenny have to create this cradle for their family. The Second Vatican Council states clearly:

> Since parents have given children their life, they are bound by the most serious obligation to educate their offspring and therefore must be recognized as the primary and principal educators.... Parents are the ones who must create a family atmosphere animated by love and respect for God and man, in which the well-rounded personal and social education of children is fostered. Hence the family is the first school of the social virtues that every society needs. It is particularly in the Christian family, enriched by the grace and office of the sacrament of matrimony, that children should be taught from their early years to have a knowledge of God according to the faith received in Baptism, to worship Him, and to love their neighbor.[122]

✠　　✠　　✠

Jimmy and Jenny spend hours teaching Johnny how to eat, walk, talk, use the toilet, and so forth. Likewise, they are to teach their child the ways of God as a member of the Catholic Church. They do so by the way they relate to each other, to their child, and to other people, especially his grandparents and relatives. Johnny begins to perceive good behavior during the process of socialization. But there are also words and gestures

---

[121] Francis, *Amoris laetitia*, no. 57.

[122] Vatican Council II, Declaration on Christian Education *Gravissimum educationis* (October 28, 1965), no. 3.

that teach the child how to make the Sign of the Cross, learn the names Jesus and Mary, and learn the basic Catholic prayers such as the Our Father and Hail Mary. They introduce Johnny to the Church.

I am personally not too thrilled with "cry rooms." Even a child's cry is a refreshing sound that supplies hope in that there is new life in the Church and that these are the wonderful Catholics and leaders of tomorrow. People who dismiss children from church are acting like the Lord's disciples, whom He chided for trying to get children away from Him, while the parents were pushing them toward Jesus.[123]

Jimmy and Jenny should try their best to ignore accusatory adult frowning faces. Their child belongs with them in church. This is true even if that child might be tired or hungry, and even if he must become incrementally aware of how to behave in church. It is a very slow, long, patient, persevering, and holy process.

Soon, Jimmy and Jenny will send their child to school. As loving parents, Jimmy and Jenny take time to evaluate which school Johnny should attend, for there will be long hours spent there, away from their presence and supervision. Hence, parents should thoroughly evaluate the actual content of what their child will be taught because teachers play a vital role in the education of their pupils. Thus, there should be healthy interaction, mutual support, and constructive communication between parents and teachers. They should work together as a team.[124]

The first day of school arrives. It is the first substantial separation of Johnny from his parents — he cries, the parents cry, but all

___

[123] Matt. 19:13; Mark 10:13–14; Luke 18:15.

[124] There are currently pockets in the United States where there is a major struggle between parents and teachers, in particular related to gender issues. Parents should keep in mind that the role of teachers is to collaborate and assist parents in their child's intellectual, social, emotional, and religious education. Teachers should be held accountable for what they teach, and be challenged when their own personal values, beliefs, and agendas go against the religious beliefs of their pupils and their families.

will be well at the end of the day. Little Johnny stands as a reminder to all parents that a child is truly a gift from God. In a way, by entrusting them with this young child, God is also entrusting them with the future of the Church and society!

The Second Vatican Council calls the family the "domestic church,"[125] reminding young parents that their home is a dwelling place for the Lord Who constantly assists them in becoming holier and more genuine contributors to the Church and society at large.

[125] *Lumen gentium*, no. 11. See also, *Familiaris consortio*, nos. 11, 49, 51, 59, 61, 65.

A Rainbow Moment

As he continues to grow and learn, Johnny's parents fondly recall the joy of discovering that they were to become parents. And as they continue to work together as a team, Jimmy and Jenny inspire other parents to do the same, loving one another, supporting one another, and finding time to be with one another as they face together the demands and responsibilities of their noble vocation as parents. This calls for a united heart and mind; for approaching difficulties as a unit; for taking care of one another's needs and not only of their baby's; for counteracting our contemporary culture's idol of individualism and recognizing it as a real enemy to their marriage and family; and for calling on the Lord and Our Lady at least daily as they teach their child the tenets of the precious gift of faith. Thus, thanks to little Johnny, something amazing happens on their way to Heaven—God sends another rainbow.

CHAPTER TWELVE

The Entire Person

AS A SCHOOLBOY, JOHNNY'S motor skills become smoother and stronger. He learns how to write neatly; is involved in choosing to wear appropriate clothing; and does some house chores such as keeping his room clean, making his own bed, and helping to wash dishes. He begins to read stories rather than simply identify words; his knowledge of language grows as he learns grammar and expands his vocabulary. This is also the time when Johnny may be taught how to use a cell phone or a computer responsibly, and how to control them rather than be controlled by them. In other words, he begins to develop personal responsibility.

Johnny also begins to experience growing up physically, especially as he approaches puberty; he gains weight and sheds baby fat. He soon develops sexual characteristics and becomes more aware of belonging to a group outside his immediate family. He begins to experience peer pressure, which pushes him to behave, dress, and have toys and gadgets similar to his peers'. Without attaching any nuance to morality, he might begin lying, try cheating, and consider stealing. This is usually where most child psychologists stop. They fail to take into account the totality of Johnny as a human being — that he needs not only a social code but a moral code as well.

Johnny's experiences in his first five years have a very important effect on his development later in life. His parents play the crucial role during this time. Some child psychologists propose that there are five developmental stages between birth and age five, stages that are not only physical, but also social, emotional, cognitive, and communicative. They advocate, and rightly so, that Johnny's early childhood development is critical because it lays the foundation for the rest of his life which will involve behavior, social skills, establishing emotional boundaries, getting along with his siblings and other children, forming close relationships and intimacy, the openness to be schooled, and an ensuing sense of achievement.[126]

However, these experts leave out one major ingredient: incremental spiritual growth. This is also an important aspect of human development, which many psychological approaches fail to take into account in evaluating a child past the age of five, when the child begins to reach the age of reason. Does this mean that such behavioral experts do not believe in our spiritual side or do not think it is important for an individual? If this is the case, then they fail to render a great service to the individual, for even creation itself calls out to its Creator.

Psalm 19 opens with the words: "Heaven tells the glory of God and the firmament shows the work of His hands."[127] A similar declaration is found in Psalm 50: "The heavens proclaim His justice, for God Himself is Judge."[128] When the pious Jew looked at creation, he was overwhelmed with how God made man and woman its center. This great wonder is proclaimed in Psalm 8: "Lord, our Lord, how majestic is Your Name in all the earth.... When I consider the heavens, the work of Your hands, the moon and the stars which You have arranged, what is man

---

[126] Rosalyn Sword, "Why Is Child Development So Important in Early Years?," High Speed Training, January 15, 2021, https://www.highspeed-training.co.uk/hub/child-development-in-early-years/.

[127] Ps. 19:2.

[128] Ps. 50:6.

that You keep him in mind, mortal man that You care for him?... You have made him lord over the works of Your hands, putting all things under his feet."[129] How can a professional miss this universal declaration and still claim to privately respect Christian or Jewish values?

Time passes, and soon Johnny is thirteen and officially a teenager. This is a critical stage of his life: he has to deal with puberty; with hormones going wild; with an increasing desire for privacy and independence. Johnny strives to break free from the expectations of his parents by showing he is a nonconformist, all the while trying very hard to conform with his peers. Johnny has moments of rebellion, sulking, depression, feelings of rejection and abandonment, and he is very touchy and temperamental. He tests boundaries, while seeing his loving and concerned parents as interfering in his private life, personal decisions, and the company he keeps. He is in desperate need of acceptance and affirmation from any source.

These are mostly unknown waters for parents and child alike. One might say that Johnny is an experiment both for himself and for his parents because as Johnny gets more independent, his relationship with his parents changes. All of this requires a great emotional adjustment on the part of the parents. Thankfully, it will pass as he grows older and matures.

Many parents dread the onset of these teen years, which present great challenges as their children begin copying their peers and become less dependent on their parents. Some parents have the mistaken idea that the best way to make their child conform is to send him to some

---

129 Ps. 8:1, 4–5, 7.

professional counseling. Though this might be a good idea in some instances, it must not detach or emotionally separate parents from their growing child. Meanwhile, they should continue to show their support and their love. There needs to be constant communication.

Jimmy and Jenny must be very patient, forgiving, and good listeners. Teenage Johnny may feel that his ideas and feelings do not matter to his parents and that they never listen to him, whereas they always insist that he listen to them and follow their "orders." Jimmy and Jenny wonder at times what has happened to their sweet child, forgetting that they themselves went through this phase years ago. Perhaps this is a time when Jimmy and Jenny, as parents, should allow their son to teach them how to listen to him; to make them feel what he feels and understand what is important to him; to show him respect and allow him to teach them how to express it. In a way Johnny, the son, becomes the teacher of his parents.

The physical, social, emotional, cognitive, communicative, and spiritual phases of development associated with the teenage years can create special challenges for parents, who must remember that their child has to grow as a *total* person. Teenagers need opportunities and assistance to grow spiritually as well. The spiritual foundations Jimmy and Jenny have given their son will need to ripen and deepen into an adult faith. In this, Johnny is in a better place than that of his peers whose parents failed to provide for their child's spiritual development, including Baptism, having determined that their child will make that choice at a later age. How absurd! They would never apply this to any other part of their child's development—his physical, or emotional, or intellectual growth. Why should they not guide his spiritual development as well?

We know that Baptism makes us children of God and members of His household. When Johnny was conceived, he received his human nature from his parents. When he was baptized, he received a share of the divine nature from God Himself. This is why Baptism is referred to as rebirth as a child of God. In his Letter to the Galatians, St. Paul declares: "All of you are children of God through faith in Jesus Christ. All of you who were baptized into the Lord Jesus have clothed yourselves with Christ."[130]

Just as Johnny's parents must reflect on whether they are taking God into account in their personal lives and that of their child, so must we consider the same question for the young people in our lives: Are we giving them the example they need to follow?

As Johnny begins to understand the difference between good and evil, and as he learns to distinguish between morally good and bad choices (and their respective consequences), Jimmy and Jenny must continue to remind their son what is good and what is bad, what pleases the Lord and what makes Him sad. They will remind him to avoid bad company; to avoid drugs and smoking; to tell them if he was touched inappropriately. They teach him about his guardian angel whom God assigned specifically to him to help and protect him.

They also teach him to give and receive forgiveness, and especially the freedom that he can receive in the Sacrament of Reconciliation, where his sins are wiped away each time he tells Jesus that he is really sorry and asks Him to help him change.

His parents pray with Johnny, both individually and together. They encourage him to pray on his own as well, at the beginning and end of the day, before and after meals, and when he does not know what to do or how to behave. They teach him how to comport himself in church, and how to always have good manners. This is a very long and complicated process for both Johnny and his parents. However, Jimmy and Jenny are to be there for their growing son and to provide him with a good sense of being loved, of feeling safe, and of being supported and trusted.

---

[130] Gal. 3:26–27. See also John 1:12; Rom. 8:14, 16.

When Teenage Johnny does things to press his parents' panic button, they learn to press the prayer button. Jimmy and Jenny know that God did not only entrust their son to them, but remains with all of them, and is ever ready to assist with His grace. It is not just a matter of parents asking God to make Johnny internally peaceful — they must follow up with concrete acts. They should never give up on prayer and on practicing their faith. So when Johnny wants to sleep in on Sundays and forego going to Mass with them, Jimmy and Jenny should not insist that he join them. Rather, they should tell him that they are going to Mass and ask if he wishes to join them and his younger siblings. Thus, Johnny feels that he is the one who makes the decision.

A Rainbow Moment

It is important that young families establish regular family prayer time and continue the habit as part of their lives both individually and as a family. Regular family prayer should not be suspended, as if the family is giving up on prayer and reliance on God for a while. Rather, let each family member take turns saying the prayer before meals and another one the prayer after meals. Recite the Rosary together—if not a whole Rosary, at least a decade or a couple of Hail Marys as a family. The Venerable Fr. Patrick Peyton, C.S.C., who fervently promoted the family Rosary, never tired of saying that "the family that prays together stays together."

Good things catch on, and other parents and young families will be able to detect that there is something special in Johnny's family. They might even become inquisitive about what ticks in Johnny's family. In this regard, Jimmy, Jenny, and Johnny become concrete Catholic witnesses. So something mighty amazing happens on our way to Heaven—God extends another rainbow.

CHAPTER THIRTEEN

A Domestic Church

EVEN WHEN HE OR she is physically an adult, a teenager has a long way to go to be fully developed emotionally and cognitively. The timing of physical and cognitive changes varies from one person to the next throughout adolescence, each at their own pace and in their own time. The famous boxer Muhammed Ali once stated, "The man who views the world at 50 the same as he did at 20 has wasted 30 years of his life." The Gospel of St. Luke tells us that after Mary and Joseph found Jesus in the Temple, and the three returned home, and "Jesus kept on growing wiser and more mature."[131]

As Johnny matures and advances toward adulthood, he longs for greater and greater autonomy. However, he needs a curfew when he goes out with friends, and he remains accountable to his parents for his whereabouts as long as he still lives at home. He has come a very long way from when, as a baby, he depended on others simply to move a few inches from point A to point B. Now he is not only able to move long distances with his feet or on a bicycle, but he can operate a motorcycle or car. And yet his brain is still growing, and he needs continued guidance as he learns to cross a busy street or to make a left-hand turn with oncoming traffic.

[131] Luke 2:52.

Just as he gradually gains greater physical autonomy, Johnny will need to acquire more and more psychological autonomy as he sets independent judgments and opinions and, as psychologists and psychiatrists advocate, works out his own principles of right and wrong. As he experiences spiritual growth, Johnny learns that there is an objective moral code — something that is not centered on oneself but on the common good. The cradle of this spiritual growth and discipline to live according to Christian mores is not an academic school but the school of life — Johnny's home. As stated earlier, it is the domestic church.[132]

Of course, there are other people and resources to help instill moral values in Johnny: Sacred Scripture, the teachings of the Church, teachers, priests and religious, the lives of saints, religious instruction outside the home, and so forth. Pope Francis states that "The Church is called to cooperate with parents through suitable pastoral initiatives, assisting them in the fulfilment of their educational mission. She must always do this by helping them to appreciate their proper role and to realize that by their reception of the sacrament of marriage they become ministers of their children's education. In educating them, they build up the Church."[133] He goes on to state, "The Church is a family of families, constantly enriched by the lives of all those domestic churches."[134]

Of course, Johnny first received his basic knowledge of right and wrong through his parents' concrete example, watching what they do and say. This kind of parental teaching and instruction has gone on for many years, assisted at the proper time by others, especially teachers. However, teachers never replace Jimmy and Jenny as

---

[132] See chap. 11. See also *Lumen gentium*, no. 11. See also *Familiaris consortio*, nos. 11, 49, 51, 59, 61, 65; CCC 2223.

[133] *Amoris laetitia*, no. 85. See also *Familiaris consortio*, no. 38.

[134] *Amoris laetitia*, no. 87. See also, *Familiaris consortio*, nos. 11, 49, 51, 59, 61, 65.

Johnny's primary and principal educators. Teachers do not replace parents' inalienable right and duty to educate their children.[135]

Furthermore, the family — that is, the domestic church — is the first school of essential social virtues, where each person learns to help others and serve the common good.[136] This teaching, put forward in 1965 by the Second Vatican Council, is often replaced in this day and age with the cult of individualism and tolerance, even in the classroom. We read and hear about teachers who insist on choosing their own curriculum and its contents, especially related to gender and sexual issues, irrespective of what parents want their children to be taught. This, too, is another version of individualism, and ignores completely the common good.

When this happens, parents must speak up as their children's first and primary educators. It is necessary to have an ongoing open and honest communication between parents and teachers; utter respect of each individual's role; positive interaction; attentive listening and sharing of ideas and goals; clearly set boundaries of the respective responsibilities of parents and teachers; courteous challenges of issues regarding a child's education; and a constant reminder that Divine Providence has entrusted these adults, be they parents or teachers, with the future of society.

Adolescents, like adults, need to know that they are loved, trusted, and appreciated. They also need to be reassured that they are capable of sharing affection in intimate relationships. By the time Johnny is ready to begin dating, Jimmy or Jenny will have explained to their son the difference between intimacy and sexual activity, the role of the

---

[135] *Gravissimum educationis*, no. 6.
[136] Ibid., no. 3.

virtue of purity, and the fact that sexuality is a gift from God. Just as importantly, they will have given their son the emotional support and encouragement he needs to make confident choices and withstand negative peer pressure.

One of the most important messages a parent needs to convey to their young adult children is the difference between physical and emotional intimacy. Many people today wrongly equate intimacy with sexual activity. However, these two things are not the same. Emotional intimacy belongs within close relationships in which people are open, honest, caring, respectful, and trusting. This is first learned from parents and close friendships. Neither boys nor girls go to bed with their intimate friends, for such intimacy should not promote or include a sexual relationship.

One of the most essential characteristics of emotional intimacy is the ability to communicate openly and honestly. This is something that is especially important to cultivate between parents and their adolescent and young adult children. For example, if eighteen-year-old Johnny does not mention to his parents that he is dating a certain girl, this indicates that something is amiss and that communication between him and his parents needs to improve.

God prohibits casual and recreational sexual activity. Virtuous pure intimacy and respect for the other person are essential to cultivate in romantic relationships. On the other hand, children brought up in a home where closeness is lacking or where interpersonal relationships in their proper family are distorted, such as where there is a physical and/or emotional abuse, end up having very serious difficulties in learning and being comfortable with self-disclosure and self-expression because they are afraid of being rejected or hurt. Yet self-disclosure and self-expression are the foundation for intimacy.

On the other hand, when spiritual intimacy is present in a family — when they have cultivated a prayer life and built a relationship with God and the Church — it becomes easier to navigate the emotional challenges of life. When spiritual intimacy is present, Johnny will not fall completely apart or spiral into depression when a relationship falters. He will recover because he has not lost self-worth; he is dating for a simple purpose: God helping him to discern and find the right future spouse. Of course, he will feel very hurt and somewhat depressed, but he will also be comforted with the fact that he has a wholesome future and can count on the support of his parents and significant people in his young life.

There will also be times when Johnny is relieved that his romantic relationship is over, for he had already concluded that it is either not good for him or toxic, but did not know how to bring it to closure. Once again, Johnny has to rely on his parents' wise input and his spiritual life and values in confronting such a situation. Peers can provide emotional support, but not wise counsel.

Throughout his adolescence, Johnny's peers and parents witness that maturing is a lifelong and challenging process. No one can be pushed into maturing, for no one is a lump of clay in one's parents' hands. Johnny reminds parents to be loving, supporting, very patient, understanding, and always forgiving. He reminds them that mistakes are part of growth, and that a relapse in his behavior or judgment is an opportunity to learn and move forward in the right direction. He reminds them that God has taken a gamble and assigned this specific child to his or her specific parents. He reminds them that a solid spiritual life sustains both the adolescent and the parents.

At the same time, Jimmy and Jenny are also growing as parents. Daily they are reminded that everyone is imperfect; that all of us make big and small mistakes; and that if we fail, we should never give up and should continue seeking the Lord's help and the guidance of the Holy Spirit. As Johnny's parents prepare their child for an adult

Christian life, they must allow their adolescent child to learn from his mistakes. Johnny and his parents remind families of the great importance of ongoing and honest communication. He challenges those in his age group and their respective parents to take stock and evaluate their relationship as children of God. St. Paul tells the child to "obey your parents for this is pleasing to God."[137] On the other hand, in the same breath he directs parents how to relate to their children: "Parents, do not provoke your children, lest they might give up."[138] Jimmy, Jenny, and their son Johnny invite parents to reflect on how active God is in their personal life and family and whether they have shut to Him the doors of their hearts and minds. The three challenge families to turn their home into a domestic church, a place where they can sit down together as a family to try to sort out things out together — seeking the assistance of professional help when needed.

As their children grow, parents remain the primary and principal educators; teachers and counselors are there to assist, so parents and educators are to have mutual respect and cooperation in the intellectual, emotional, and spiritual formation of the young person. Parent-teacher communication is essential for the sake of the child. Parents disgruntled with the educational system are reminded not to fall into the idol of individualism and exceedingly insist on personal rights at the cost of the common good. Parents must not expect teachers to be the "fixers" of their child's emotional or social problems, however, because the formation of the young person begins at home.

---

[137] Col. 3:20. See also Eph. 6:1.
[138] Col. 3:21. See also Eph. 6:4.

A Rainbow Moment

When their child begins dating, parents must continue showing their love and support. They must show that they trust his or her judgment, knowing he has received a sound moral education at home. Even when adolescents make mistakes and experience the consequences of those mistakes, our role shifts. Our ability to control actions and outcomes is limited; now we must entrust our loved ones to God, and become that adolescent's wise and trusted guide rather than their friend at all costs. Together, we continue our journey, prayerfully and lovingly, always with one eye out for a heavenly rainbow, looking for the amazing things that happen on our way to Heaven.

CHAPTER FOURTEEN

Grandparenting

JOHNNY AND JOSEY'S WEDDING day has arrived. It is a memorable and joy-filled day for them and for their respective families and friends. It is also an occasion when the newlyweds' union reflects the unbreakable and self-giving union between Christ and His Church. As Pope Francis once stated, "The Church received from her Lord the mission of proclaiming the Good News, and she also illuminates and supports that 'great mystery' which is conjugal and family love. The Church as a whole can be said to be a big family, and, in a very particular way through the life of those who form a domestic church, she receives and transmits the light of Christ and his Gospel in the family sphere."[139]

Very soon, Johnny and Josey will make grandparents of their respective parents by the arrival of their first bundle of joy, Judy. The next significant issue for Johnny and Josey is to determine the role of grandparents in their family.

The Old Testament prophet Joel, in a few powerful words, links three generations: grandparents, parents, and grandchildren. He proclaims: "Your sons and your daughters shall prophesy and your old shall dream dreams and your young shall see visions."[140] These

---

[139] Francis, Address to the Officials of the Tribunal of the Roman Rota for the Inauguration of the Judicial Year (January 27, 2023).

[140] Joel 2:28. See also Acts 2:17.

words, to a certain extent, can be analogously applied to Johnny and Josey as parents who work to have harmony in their young family. The words may also be applied to the role that grandparents play in the lives of their grandchildren. It entails the presence of an ongoing and enriching encounter among the three generations.

Our Lord had maternal grandparents: Our Lady's parents, Joachim and Anne, the patron saints of grandparents.[141] We know their names and where they lived, Nazareth, from sources outside the New Testament.[142]

The Gospel of St. Luke informs us that Our Lady lived in Nazareth when the Annunciation took place.[143] Mary was a young adolescent virgin, living at the house of her parents, when the Archangel Gabriel was sent by God to invite her to become the mother of His Only Son. The same Gospel informs us that Mary and Joseph, now married, went from Nazareth to register in Bethlehem, as demanded by the Roman census.[144]

The Gospel of St. Matthew narrates how an angel appeared to St. Joseph in a dream and instructed him to flee with Mary and Jesus to Egypt because King Herod, envious and paranoid, was seeking the baby's death. Following the death of Herod an angel, in another dream, directed St. Joseph to take his wife and her child back to Palestine, and the Holy Family settled in Nazareth.[145] So, they went back to Our Lady's hometown, and it is reasonable to assume that Joachim and Anne were still alive. It is also reasonable to assume that the

---

[141] The Church has designated July 26 as the feast day of Sts. Joachim and Anne.

[142] The names of Our Lady's parents first appear in the non-inspired (apocryphal) *Gospel of James*. They are not mentioned in the divinely inspired Sacred Scriptures.

[143] Luke 1:26–38.

[144] Ibid., 2:4.

[145] Matt. 2:13–15; 19–23.

Lord's maternal grandparents were involved in the life of the toddler Jesus, for by now the Lord was about two or three years old. So there was an ongoing encounter among the three generations as long as the Lord's maternal grandparents lived. Each family is invited to duplicate this beautiful, harmonious relationship.

One positive side effect of trying economic times is that adult children may return to their parental home, having left it to establish their own life independent of their parents. Granted, this relocation requires great adjustment on the part of all involved, but it carries with it many hidden blessings. For many decades, the American household was perceived as a place that children were expected to leave around age eighteen, whether to go to college or seek work or join the Armed Forces. Moving away from home to establish financial independence near the end of the teen years was deemed something good and mature. But is it?

The model of extended families living together was replaced by a nuclear family, devoid of the involvement of grandparents. In addition, the prevalence of automobiles and other forms of transportation made it easier to travel to faraway places. And yet this mobility came at a cost: the beginning of the collapse of the extended family unit, where much support was offered. Granted, some children were better off being away from their dysfunctional families, but most of the families, despite tensions and disagreements, were enriching to all their members. This nuclear family soon gave rise to the "empty nest syndrome," describing the grief and sense of loneliness that many parents experience when their children, especially if they have one child, move out of the home.[146] Granted, many parents and children keep regularly in touch

---

[146] A. Bougea et al., "Empty-Nest-Related Psychosocial Stress: Conceptual Issues, Future Directions in Economic Crisis," *Psychiatriki* 30 (2019): 329–338, https://www.psychiatriki-journal.gr/documents/psychiatry/30.4-EN-2019-329.pdf.

with one another through phone calls or video calls, as well as the occasional holiday visits. But the ongoing emotional support is minimized because of the lack of a constant physical presence.

Johnny and Josey decide to establish their home near Johnny's parents, emulating Our Lady and St. Joseph, who did not hoard their son Jesus but shared Him with others, first with the poor shepherds of Bethlehem[147] and then with the Wise Men from the East.[148] Jimmy and Jenny, unlike the Wise Men, will not give gold, frankincense, and myrrh to Judy. Their gifts are love, care, helping Josey in keeping Judy clean and dressed, babysitting, helping Judy to walk and to talk, being their granddaughter's playmates, helping Judy's parents to spend time together, accompanying Josey to the doctor when Judy needs checkups or is sick, lulling the crying baby to sleep, helping with the never-ending washing of baby laundry, and many other things. Jimmy and Jenny also provide emotional support to the new parents and, without being intrusive, also offer parental advice when asked. All of these things become more important with the arrival of Judy's siblings.

One of the greatest gifts that Jenny will give her granddaughter is teaching her about the Catholic Faith and helping Josey to teach little Judy short Catholic prayers. The grandparents might occasionally adjust their Mass schedule by babysitting Judy when she is under the weather, so Johnny and Josey can worship at their parish church. Of course, there will be moments of tension because the young parents might feel that the grandparents have overstepped their boundaries. However, this should always be resolved by healthy, open, and positive communication. The grandparents, like the new parents, dream dreams about Judy's future, and only want the best for her.

---

[147] Luke 2:8–20.
[148] Matt. 2:1–2, 11.

In addition to practical help, such as cooking or warming Judy's milk, Jimmy and Jenny will help their children grow in their own role as young parents by listening to their worries and soothing and reassuring them. At every phase of their granddaughter's young life, there will be new opportunities to lend support. As Judy begins school, Jimmy and Jenny might help by reading to her or telling her stories that capture her short attention span. When Judy gets older, the grandparents might also help in resolving some tension between her and her parents. One cannot quantify the influence of the special connection between grandchildren and their grandparents, but it is an established fact that having actively involved grandparents does help children grow in confidence, cope with stress, and have fewer behavioral issues as they get older. They might also go to their grandparents to seek advice and/or comfort.

Of course, the most important thing for Judy's psychological makeup is that she feels loved by her parents and grandparents. Babies, toddlers, and preschool children learn and grow through a close, loving, and caring relationship with adults, especially their parents, and next in line with their grandparents. Judy is made to feel safe and secure in the process of socialization.

Children are not to be hoarded but are to be loved by other people, especially grandparents. The arrival of Judy is a wonderful event in the life of the new parents, but it is also such for the grandparents and extended family. Young families are invited to reflect on how they are relating to their parents and how they are allowing access to the grandparents and their extended family to the life of their child. This involvement may be a true gift not only to the grandchild but also to the parents. It should be kept in mind that there is a very subtle teaching going on: the way Johnny and Josey relate to Jimmy and Jenny will indicate to their children the way they should treat their parents when they reach their grandparents' age.

Young parents must never use their child to either reward or punish the grandparents when there is discord. A child should not be denied love and care just because there is a disagreement between her parents and their parents. This is surely not part of God's plan for families. Loving and caring for a child involves hard work, moving in the same direction for the sake of the child, a lot of diplomacy, resolving issues through healthy communication and accommodation, putting aside personal grudges and resentment, establishing clear and sustainable boundaries, and putting family harmony as one big priority.

In a way, all of this goes back to St. Paul's definition of love: "Love is patient and kind; love does not envy; love is not upset neither conceited. Love is not rude, neither does it seek its own; it is not self-seeking, neither does it entertain a wrong suffered, does not delight in iniquity. Love never gives up, never loses faith, is always hopeful, and endures through every circumstance."[149] This is to be practiced not only between the spouses, but also among family members. It might prove to be occasionally very difficult and tense, but is not this why we should ask all the more for God's assistance and that of the Holy Family?

Johnny and Josey as well as their parents have dreams for little Judy that cannot be achieved without mutual loving, respectful, and caring cooperation. There will be times when each of them has to bite his or her tongue and not make an issue of something that turns out to be unimportant in the long run. Hence, they should call on the Holy Spirit and their individual guardian angel to assist them in discerning or interpreting the value of what is being shared.

[149] 1 Cor. 13:4–7.

A Rainbow Moment

Grandparents have a special role to play in the lives of their grandchildren—and in the lives of the child's parents. It's important to resist the tendency in our throwaway culture to minimize the importance of such vital relationships. Grandparents are to be greatly valued because they can make a huge positive influence in the life of a grandchild; their long experience is a source of wisdom which should be welcomed rather than dismissed or avoided; and they can provide much support and assistance to young parents. Thus, when applied to grandparents, we refer to the Psalmist who says: "They still bear fruit in old age. They will flourish and be vital and fresh, rich in trust and love and contentment,"[150] and in another psalm: "Do not cast me off at the time of old age."[151]

By the way they live their lives, Jimmy and Jenny remind their contemporaries that an involved extended family is healthy, though boundaries are to be respected. The dynamics within the family and in their relationships reveal the hidden treasures that may be found planted inside the life and experience of older people. When these things are present, something amazing happens on our way to Heaven: the appearance of another divine rainbow.

[150] Ps. 92:14.
[151] Ps. 71:9.

CHAPTER FIFTEEN

Suffering Together

THERE IS AN OLD and true saying: bad things happen to good people. Johnny's younger sister Connie is a great, vibrant, and self-giving person. She has remained single and lives with her parents, Jimmy and Jenny. Then one day she is diagnosed with ovarian cancer.

Naturally, all are frightened and stressed by this very tragic news, especially Connie. She begins chemo immediately — and so do the intense sufferings and problems for Connie, which go hand in hand with such aggressive treatment.

Her entire family offers prayers and words of comfort, proposing to help in whatever way they can; they are united in great love and pain. Looking for a miracle, they seek the assistance of all the saints in Heaven. Masses for Connie's healing are celebrated. Her name is added to the Prayers of the Faithful at Mass. Candles are lit, as hands and hearts are joined in prayer for Connie.

Slowly and gradually, Connie comes to realize that this is God's mysterious will for her, the means by which she will go to Heaven. This realization brings emotional ups and downs, fleeting anger, occasional depressive moments, bitter tears, and cries from the heart. God understands why she feels this way; this is a very heavy cross to bear.

In time, Connie and the family, holding on to their faith, begin to accept harsh reality. Eventually, there is the peace of resignation, accepting whatever God sends Connie. Frequently she prays with the Psalmist: "My soul, give thanks to the Lord, all my being, bless His holy name. My soul, give thanks to the Lord and never forget how kind He has been."[152]

✠　　✠　　✠

The Book of Job broaches the subject of suffering, though it does not answer all our questions. No one on earth can provide an adequate answer to suffering. Of course, every sick person wants to be healed, especially those who suffer from chronic pain or terminal illness. I personally think that terminally sick people are blessed and lucky in that God has provided time for them to prepare themselves to meet Him face-to-face.

Many of us experience "growing pains" as a sign that we are physically growing. I remember this taking place when I was a boy and was growing tall "too fast" — a positive sign of growth. However, there are also many other kinds of negative suffering, such as emotional or mental suffering. This kind of suffering is generally unwelcome, and most people believe such suffering is undeserved. When they encounter it, some people become deeply shaken in their faith and trust in a loving God, and they ask themselves if this suffering is due to some terrible thing that they have done. They wonder if God is somehow punishing them. This is far from the truth. Pain and suffering, like death, entered human life with Original Sin.[153]

Suffering of any kind can lead some to question the very existence of God, especially a God Who allows the innocent to suffer. Others become preoccupied with the fact that God does not somehow shield us from suffering from the wrongdoing of others, such as the pain brought on by those who malign people with their gossip, or who

---

[152] Ps. 103:1–2.
[153] See Gen. 3:17–19.

destroy the lives of people through Ponzi schemes, cheating, stealing, bullying, terrorizing, exploiting, abusing, and so forth. These evil people often go unpunished for their misdeeds, either permanently or for a very long time ... at least while they live on earth.

There are also sufferings that people bring upon themselves as a consequence of their bad decisions and actions: think of those who drive under the influence of alcohol and cause a major accident with severe bodily harm or even death to themselves and others, including their loved ones. God is not to blame in such situations. On the other hand, some people need to hit rock bottom to wake up and evaluate their life and irresponsible, sinful, and destructive behavior.

Not everyone is willing to face the truth or take responsibility for their actions. For some it is easier to blame others or their very flawed upbringing, and they do not see the dire need to change. And yet, there are those who learn from these consequences, are totally transformed, and seek help. In all these cases, we need God's help. We must fervently pray for the conversion of those who seem unrepentant and continue with their irresponsible and immoral behavior. We must wash ourselves in God's river of mercy, forgiveness, and healing — just as the pagan Namaan did in the River Jordan and was healed of his leprosy.[154] He had originally resisted the prophet Elisha's simple directives but eventually gave in, did what he was asked to do, and was healed. His response was something exemplary: "Now I know that there is no God in all the earth but only the One in Israel!"[155] There are many times that God asks us to do something very ordinary and simple, as was asked of Namaan, and we are healed of the leprosy of suffering and sin, and especially of our lack of trust and faith in God.

[154] 2 Kings 5:1–6; 8–14.
[155] Ibid., 5:15.

Jesus Christ understands the true purpose of our suffering. We may not understand why there is a lot of suffering in our lives and throughout the world, but we just have to look at the completely innocent and sinless crucified Jesus. He promised on the Hill of Golgotha that those who place their trust in Him will inherit an eternal future devoid of death, tears, and sufferings.

✠　　✠　　✠

Connie, Jimmy, Jenny, and the rest of the family reflect on this mystery of suffering as Connie becomes sicker and weaker. They do not understand her suffering, yet they are consoled by trust and hope. They fervently pray for a miracle, adding the clause: "If this is Your will." Their suffering continues, but there is also the accompaniment of consolation and inner peace.

Pope Francis has spoken about consolation, which is especially needed in time of great suffering: "What is spiritual consolation? It is an experience of *interior joy*, that lets [us] see God's presence in all things. It strengthens faith and hope, and even the ability to do good. The person who experiences consolation never gives up in the face of difficulties because he or she always experiences a peace that is stronger than the trial. It is, therefore, a tremendous gift for the spiritual life as well as life in general … and to live this interior joy."[156] Yes, it is true that one can experience inner joy and peace even in the deepest throes of suffering.

The tragically sick Connie, as well as Jimmy, Jenny, and their entire family, are witnesses to suffering, especially for those who have very sick small children. Inviting them to allow God into their lives and into their pain and misery, they assure those who suffer that God

---

[156] Francis, General Audience (November 23, 2022).

will help them cope if them allow Him to enter their lives. They do not promise a healing miracle, only inner peace.

Yes, many tears will be shed, much suffering will be experienced, and many moments of crisis will come their way. In all these things, God will console them and draw them closer to His heart.

✠　✠　✠

Connie gets increasingly sick. Chemo is not doing its work, and the cancer spreads and becomes metastasized. Even when there is nothing more the doctors can do for her, Connie is receiving spiritual assistance through prayers and sacraments, especially through the reception of the Holy Eucharist and the Sacrament of the Sick, a most powerful sacrament to strengthen those on their way to God.

Some people go to extremes to escape the process of aging and even death itself. Yet, no living person will escape illness and aging, which allude to our mortality and eventual death. This is the unchangeable law of human nature. Still, since the Lord wants to be with us especially when we are sick, He established the Sacrament of the Anointing of the Sick. It confers a special grace on its recipient.

Jesus alluded to this sacrament when He sent the Twelve Apostles on a mission to preach repentance. During this mission, they anointed sick people with oil, and many were healed.[157] Later, after the Lord's Ascension, the Apostle James, inspired by the Lord's directives, recommended and encouraged the calling of Church elders to anoint a sick person in the name of the Lord and to pray over the individual.[158] Priests and bishops have been anointing and praying over the sick since that time. Only a validly ordained priest or bishop may administer this sacrament because it involves the sacramental

---

[157]　See Mark 6:7–13.
[158]　See James 5:14–16.

absolution of sins. This sacrament reflects the fact that Jesus not only healed the sick but also forgave their sins.[159] In other words, He healed the whole person.[160] Thus, the Church recommends that whenever possible, the Anointing of the Sick should include the Sacrament of Penance and Reconciliation as well as Holy Communion.

Connie, Jimmy, Jenny, and their family find the purpose of all of their suffering in the crucified Christ. He suffered not for His own sake, but for our sake. However, Connie suffers not only for the sanctification of herself but also of others and the Church.[161] The same applies to her loving family. The underlying aim is that our personal suffering should be joined to the sufferings of the Lord, instead of us becoming self-absorbed. [162] The Anointing of the Sick provides us with an opportunity of acquiring a Christ-oriented mindset.

[159] See Mark 2:5–12.
[160] Ibid., 2:17.
[161] *Lumen gentium*, IV no. 31.
[162] See Matt. 8:17; Isa. 53:4.

A Rainbow Moment

In 1972, Pope St. Paul VI introduced changes in the administration of this sacrament, allowing its administration also when a person is gravely ill, when one's physical condition worsens, or due to old age. Thus, we may receive the Anointing of the Sick a number of times during our lifetime.[163] Jesus and the Church wish to accompany every sick brother and sister, recalling the Lord's words: "Come to me, all who labor and are forced to bear heavy burdens, and I will give you rest."[164]

The aim of this sacrament entails our whole person, body and soul. It aims at strengthening us during some kind of serious illness and restoring our spiritual health through the absolution of our sins. There are also times when a sick person is healed.

This sacrament is always associated with the Passion, Death, and Resurrection of the Lord. The special sacramental grace bestowed on those who receive the sacrament unites them to the sufferings of the Lord for their own good and that of the Church; gives them strength, inner peace, and courage to endure suffering in a Christian way; forgives their sins if they are unable to celebrate the Sacrament of Penance and Reconciliation;

---

163 Paul VI, Apostolic Constitution *Sacram unctione infirmorum* (November 30, 1972).

164 Matt. 11:28.

seeks healing of mind and body if this is in accordance with God's will; prepares them for eternal life; and, whenever possible, allows them to receive the Lord in the Eucharist for the last time in the form of Viaticum. The Lord, accompanied by Our Lady, St. Joseph, the Communion of Saints, and the angels, is present at the moment of a person's death. Connie and her family are never alone, even if no other human being is physically present. Her dealing with her profound sufferings is a great Christian witness.

We must all seek the Lord when we or a loved one is sick. Yes, many tears are shed, many moments are spent in fear and apprehension, and endless days are spent in great pain. However, we do not travel alone, nor are we abandoned to a devastating disease and suffering. The Lord and the Church walk with us to sustain us, to comfort us, and to provide us with inner tranquility. Our prayers are answered, not according to our plans but according to God's will. This faith-filled approach replaces fear with trust in God. This is not an easy process, but it can be done when we allow God into our inner life. We must unite with our loved one, emotionally and prayerfully, in order to make our way along this road of suffering, which is very rough and cannot be traveled alone.

Connie reminds us that illness is not a punishment from God but is part and parcel of living as fallen children

of God, deeply wounded but resilient with
God's assistance. We are reminded that although
we cannot understand suffering, we can cope with it as
we look at the Lord on the Cross. Even in the "valley of
the shadow of death,"[165] another rainbow is given by God,
and something amazing happens on our way to Heaven.

[165] Ps. 23:4.

CHAPTER SIXTEEN

Facing Death

THE GYNECOLOGICAL ONCOLOGIST MEETS Connie's family in one of the empty rooms at the hospital. He wants to speak with them in person about Connie. The update is terrible. The aggressive chemotherapy has failed. He tells them that some of them might have noticed that Connie was going in and out of consciousness. Some family members tell him that her occasional smile and whispered words are slowly disappearing. It is decided that she will receive only palliative care to make her comfortable, along with tubal nourishment and oxygen. She does not deserve this fate, but nonetheless it is very real. It is one of the greatest misfortunes of human life.

The following day, Jimmy, Jenny, and the rest of the heartbroken family decide that Connie should be taken home and given hospice care. Their trust in God's love and the fact that He takes care of His own does not take away their great suffering, but they do allow the Lord to help them deal with this dreadful situation. They feel powerless on the physical level, but they are equipped with the weapons of God's graces on the spiritual level as their vigil over the dying Connie begins.

Connie's young nephews and nieces are brought in by their respective parents to see their aunt, now completely still, the oxygen mask making her breathing very labored. Each little one is lifted to kiss Aunt Connie on the forehead, as the older ones kiss her hand as a gesture of goodbye. The smaller children are very quiet and on their best behavior.

The hospice nurse looks on with genuine deep feelings. She is edified by how this Catholic family is dealing with this very painful situation. She wonders what makes them behave in such a way.

Fr. Nate is called to administer to Connie the Sacrament of the Sick one last time, including the Viaticum and prayers for the dying. He includes a plenary indulgence at the end of the celebration, asking God to take this gentle soul directly to Heaven. The family joins Fr. Nate in the prayers for the dying; they have already decided that one of them will be constantly present with Connie, praying to St. Joseph to give her a saintly death and to Our Lady to accompany her to Heaven. Every thirty minutes, there is the recitation of the Rosary to pray for Connie for what remains of her earthly time.

Jimmy is the first to spend prayerful time with his daughter. Connie's agony does not last long. She gives her last breath the day after she has been taken home. Though the family has expected Connie to die soon, her death is nonetheless a shock. No one is ever really prepared for the death of a loved one. Connie's family is no exception. It truly comes "like a thief in the night."[166]

✠   ✠   ✠

Not everyone dies the way Connie does. When I used to help out as one of the chaplains at a non-Catholic hospital across from the parish rectory, I came across situations when someone greatly resisted dying, or the family would not let go. Some people are simply afraid of death because of what might happen after the moment they die. I know as a priest that this should not be so; no matter who the person is, no matter what kind of horrible life they might have led, no matter what

---

[166] Luke 12:20; 1 Thess. 5:2; 2 Pet. 3:10; Rev. 3:3; 16:15.

sins they may have committed, or how many times they rejected God, the Catholic Church teaches as truth that our loving, forgiving, and merciful God is right next to that person, inviting him or her to come back to Him, to accept His forgiveness and mercy, to be assured that he or she is still a precious son or daughter. In other words, God is offering eternal salvation.

All of us, especially those who tend to despair, need to hear and know this. If we know of someone who has given up on God for whatever reason, we should never hesitate to provide them with hope, even if we think that our words will go unheeded. We should never undermine the fact that God allows His grace and power to reach others through us. Thus, no matter what kind of spiritual state we are in, we should always allow God and His Church to speak through us by gently and opportunely stating that "God freely and abundantly forgives,"[167] for "the Lord is kind, merciful and compassionate; He is patient and His grace is abundant,"[168] and He is "ready to forgive those who call on Him."[169] All of us need to hear, as well as others to hear through us, God saying especially at the moment of our death, "Do not be afraid."

I find the Parable of the Bridegroom[170] to be very interesting regarding our moment of death. You might find it strange that I am applying this parable to death. However, if we keep in mind that the Lord is the bridegroom and we, like those five wise virgins, are waiting for His arrival, then this might make a little sense to you. The wedding feast is the celebration of the heavenly banquet. As death approaches, Christ comes to take us to the heavenly banquet, and we

---

[167] Isa. 55:7.
[168] Ps. 145:8.
[169] Ps. 86:5.
[170] Matt. 25:1–13.

await to meet Him. There are many times in the Gospel of St. Matthew that describe banquets and feasts as ongoing in Heaven.[171]

All our lives, we are constantly on a pilgrimage, or journey. We journey into the world when we leave our mother's womb. Our physical growth is an ongoing movement from infancy, to childhood, to youth, to adolescence, to young adulthood, to middle age, to old age, and finally to our physical death when the flame of our earthly journey is extinguished. But there is another journey that we undertake, and it begins at Baptism when we become God's adopted children. It is a journey of prayer and reception of various sacraments; growing and spiritually maturing through the sacraments we receive by applying them on a daily basis; moving from a lower place in our relationship with God and others to a higher and deeper one; always moving toward achieving our destiny to live with God forever in His home, for "He chose us beforehand in Him from before the creation of the world, that we shall be holy and blameless in His presence. He has constituted us in love as children of God."[172]

Connie understood that her entire life is a spiritual journey to meet the Lord, the Bridegroom, Who loves His Bride the Church, of whom Connie is a member. She has understood that Jesus, the Groom, gave Himself up due to His love for her, as St. Paul declared in his Letter to the Ephesians: "Husbands, love your wives, even as a Christ also loves His church and gave Himself up for her sake."[173] This fact provides us with our life's purpose and direction. We see this when we look at nature: just as the seed and its slow growth is ultimately judged at the time of the harvest, so is our earthly life journey of loving God and neighbor shaped and judged by its ultimate goal — meeting the Lord face-to-face. The spiritual seed was

---

[171] For example, Matt. 8:11; 22:1–14; 26:29.
[172] Eph. 1:4–5.
[173] Ibid., 5:25.

planted in our soul at our Baptism, and its slow and silent growth in sharing its light takes place by the way we live as we mature spiritually.

The symbolism of oil in our spiritual life eludes most of us due to the availability of artificial light, electricity. The purpose of oil in a lamp is to consume itself while giving light to others. Each of us is like a spiritual lamp, full of the oil of personal witness, which we give by living as brothers and sisters of Christ. Just as clay lamps come in many shapes and varieties, so do the lives of Christians, depending on their specific vocation, character, and temperament. In the end, when all is said and done, what we will be judged by is not what we have acquired but by what we have given away freely[174] through our response to God's invitation to love. Connie had walked with the Lord during life — she had achieved her life's goal with God's grace.

Connie and her family have many friends. Many of these, Catholic and non-Catholic alike, come to her Funeral Mass. Even some members of the medical profession come to show their respect and to silently state that she had touched their hearts. Fr. Nate, who celebrates Connie's Mass of Christian Burial, does not canonize Connie during his homily but speaks of her as a person who, like every person, was limited and imperfect, but who loved and served God and neighbor. She made a positive difference in the lives of many people. Subsequently, family and friends gather at the cemetery to say their last goodbye and to whisper to her, "Until we meet again in Heaven."

Connie's life, her great suffering, and her death are a concrete witness of her love for God and neighbor. Usually, she touched lives not by words but by her attitude and actions, making some people

---

[174] Matt. 6:19–21; 1 Cor. 13:2, 8–9, 13.

reflect on the fact that many a time healing miracles do not happen even to a very good and honorable person. Thanks to her love and trust in God, she helped family, friends, and medical acquaintances realize that suffering is part of living, that suffering is not a punishment from a loving God, that suffering has a purpose if it is approached the right way. Of course, being human, she was not spared moments of fear, discouragement, tears, sadness, and anxiety about the personally unknown waters she entered as her health deteriorated. But people also saw her trust in God despite what was happening in her body. Some even realized that Connie had turned her terrible pain into a prayer, despite dark moments.

Through their actions and lived witness, Connie, her parents, and their family invite onlookers to appreciate the importance of prayer and the reception of the sacraments, especially at the end of life. Connie's attitude toward her intense suffering made some people stop and reflect on their own personal suffering and how they are handling it; on their value system and what is really important in their life as they go mindlessly living each day; on what is the goal of their personal life; and on where is the place of God in their lives.

A Rainbow Moment

The Letter to the Romans tells us that "all things work for good for those who love God, who are called according to his purpose."[175] God uses even the death of those who love Him to invite those who have ignored or abandoned God out of despair to experience a feeling of hope. Perhaps this is their first inclination to change their lives for the better, having been reminded that they are not outside the reach of God's love and mercy.

As we face the end of our own lives, or the end of the life of someone dear to us, we are reminded that death is not something to be feared. Funerals and burials might present opportunities for some to think on their mortality and to come to grips with it. This is how the Lord comes to gather His own and takes them to live with Him forever. Even at the end of life, God sends another rainbow; something amazing happens on our way to Heaven.

---

[175] Rom. 8:28, NAB.

CHAPTER SEVENTEEN

Family in Crisis

JIMMY AND JENNY BEGIN to notice that their oldest grandson, fourteen-year-old Jerry, Johnny and Josey's second child, is becoming very detached and isolated from the family. At first, they attribute it to grieving for his Aunt Connie, his favorite aunt. However, as the months go by, Jerry's behavior becomes more puzzling to his grandparents, while Johnny and Josey are very busy with their younger children.

Jimmy and Jenny begin to keep a close eye on Jerry — a blessing of having grandparents involved in the lives of their grandchildren. They intensify their prayers for their grandson and make themselves more available to him. In times past, Jerry had always gone to them when he ran into trouble with his parents or had some problem with one or more of his siblings or friends. It was decided that Jerry would do his homework and studies at his grandparents' home when he was a freshman in high school so as to concentrate better by escaping the ongoing disruptions of his younger siblings. The grandparents also help him with math and English literature.

Now he begins having difficulty at school, though he has always been a great student. He begins showing disinterest in school-related activities, lacking concentration, becoming lethargic, avoiding eye contact with his grandparents, and allowing his great grades to nose-dive. He loses interest in helping his mother with chores, claiming that "this is women's stuff." He complains of being very tired and begins lagging behind in self-grooming. He stops praying and grumbles about going to church, even though he is very close to Fr. Nate. He becomes very insistent on his privacy, claims he needs less nourishment, begins losing weight, has frequent mood swings, is more irritable, and is now somewhat secretive, even with his grandparents, with whom he has always been very honest and open. His eyes also are frequently bloodshot, and he claims that this is due to lack of sleep, though, mind you, he frequently opts to stay up half the night.

Jimmy and Jenny finally decide to share their concerns with Johnny and Josey. They, too, have become alarmed by their son's pronounced behavioral and appearance changes, which they also originally attributed to grief. Johnny diplomatically checks into his son's relationship with his old friends, only to discover that Jerry is hanging around with a different group of peers. It is decided that Johnny and Josey, but particularly Johnny, should seek advice from Fr. Nate and from Dr. Louie, a close friend who is a clinical psychologist. It is concluded that Jerry might be suffering not from grieving but possibly from substance abuse.

Parents and grandparents are heartbroken and feel very guilty. Of course, Jimmy, Jenny, Fr. Nate, and Dr. Louie assure them that they have done nothing wrong: some bad things happen even to the best of families. They are told that adolescent Jerry is making some very bad decisions and failing to share his problems with either his parents or grandparents. It is decided that Johnny and Josey should first confront Jerry, and then, if there is no cooperation, Jimmy and Jenny would confront him. If neither works, Fr. Nate and Dr. Louie suggest that there be an intervention.

The following morning, Johnny tells Jerry that he should come straight home from school rather than go over to his grandparents. He obeys, showing up with bloodshot eyes and seeming somewhat lethargic. Jerry asks about his siblings, and his parents tell him that all of them are visiting with his grandparents. Johnny and Jenny ask their son to sit down. Jerry senses that his parents are very nervous and becomes suspicious. Both of them had visited the church earlier that day to ask for heavenly guidance and calmness. They have asked God to give them the right words and to help them remain calm no matter what Jerry might say or do. Nonetheless, Johnny could not concentrate at work all day long and Josey found herself crying, praying, and feeling very anxious. This is a totally new experience for them, and they are frightened.

Johnny begins the conversation by asking Jerry, "Is there is something that is bothering you?" Jerry responds with an emphatic no and asks why his dad is asking this question. Johnny explains that he and Josey have seen a big change in Jerry's behavior since the death of Aunt Connie. Jerry insists again that there is nothing wrong with him and tries to stand up. Johnny asks him to continue being seated and whispers in the depth of his heart a silent, very brief prayer to the Holy Spirit.

Jerry hesitates for a moment, then sits down again. Then Johnny tells his son that he and Josey are very concerned about him. If there is something they can do to help, they are prepared and willing to do so immediately. Jerry, from being lethargic, becomes somewhat aggressively agitated and continues to insist that there is nothing wrong with him. Josey then steps in and asks why her son's eyes are bloodshot; his great grades have gone south; he has changed his friends; he seems disinterested in being involved with his family; he does not want to go to church any longer even though he loved to go there up to Aunt Connie's death; and he is keeping mostly to himself. Jerry shouts back: "There is nothing wrong with me. What is wrong with you? Are you spying on me?" Then he marches out of the living room and runs up to his room, slamming the door.

The first round is a complete failure. Johnny and Josey are bewildered and stand silent for a minute or so. Then Johnny goes over to his parents' house to explain what has transpired and bring home the rest of the children. At first, he is greatly shaken as he tells his parents privately what has transpired, tears running down his face. Jimmy and Jenny finally manage to calm down their son, assure him that they will speak with Jerry, and tell him to wash his face before he sees the other children. It is also decided that Jerry will continue to go from school straight to his grandparents. Jimmy tells Johnny that he and Jenny will speak with Jerry after a few days and when things begin to calm down. That is exactly what happens.

Jerry goes straight from school to his grandparents the following day. On the fourth day he shows up from school with bloodshot eyes, very lethargic, and disinterested in even making an attempt to study. Jimmy and Jenny sit him down. It is now their turn to speak with their grandson. They have prayed a lot about this moment, and have consulted with Fr. Nate and Dr. Louie. They are told to be very calm, understanding, and empathic, and to avoid demanding things and instead propose options. They are to avoid mentioning the words "drugs" and "addiction" but also stick to the subject: Jerry's overall behavior.

Jerry is more receptive to his grandparents than he has been to his parents, whom he has successfully avoided for the last four days. Jimmy tells Jerry that he and his grandmother are very concerned about him because he seems to be going through a very difficult time. Jerry breaks down in tears and says that no one understands him, his parents hate him, they are spying on him, and he finds support only in his new friends. Jimmy assures Jerry that he is very much loved by his parents and all of his family. Jerry, crying, insists that his parents hate him and want to control his life though he is now a man.

Jimmy and Jenny remain quiet and well composed as they listen attentively to Jerry's list of misgivings: his parents hate him and no longer trust him, he does not like his teachers, his old friends have abandoned him, his school activities are a great pain in the neck, his parents are spying and interfering in his private life, and only his new friends understand him. He ends his narrative with sobbing.

Jimmy and Jenny simply sit quietly, allowing Jerry to finish sobbing and wiping his eyes and blowing his nose. The silence is absolute and seems to last an eternity, though in fact it lasts less than two minutes. Then Jimmy, with a very loving and compassionate tone, tells Jerry that if he would really think of what he is alleging, he might conclude that things are better than what he feels and that he will be able to give his parents a chance to prove that they really love and care about him. Jerry shakes his head repeatedly in disapproval.

Then it is Jenny's turn to speak to her grandson. She asks him if he can explain his recent behavior, which is not exactly portraying his best side. Jerry says that ever since Aunt Connie began dying, he felt betrayed by God and his aunt. Jenny does not lecture her grandson about God's love or point out that Connie did not want to be so sick or die so young. Nor does she criticize his new friends. Rather, she focuses on speaking about Jerry's great qualities, which he can still use. Jerry, still crying, hesitatingly nods his head.

Then Jenny asks him, "What can we do to help?" He responds that he will sort things out on his own. But Jenny tells her grandson that even old people cannot do that on their own most of the time. Jerry insists that he needs no help and that he is fine. Then, he walks out of the room. Once again, reaching out to Jerry has been a pronounced failure. Jimmy and Jenny conclude independently that their grandson is probably using some illegal drugs and is in dire need of help.

They remain silent for a couple of minutes, trying to absorb what has just happened. They feel discouraged and downtrodden, but not hopeless, feeling that God will help their precious grandson. Then they decide together to meet with Johnny, Josey, Fr. Nate, and Dr. Louie to see what should happen next in order to help Jerry.

Jimmy calls his son, speaks with him and Josey, and afterwards Johnny calls Fr. Nate and Dr. Louie to ask that all six of them meet. The meeting takes place the following morning. Jimmy and Johnny call their work to inform them that they will not be there the next day due to a family emergency.

The meeting takes place the following morning. It is decided that Dr. Louie would go to Jimmy's home and wait for Jerry to go there after school. Jerry is very surprised to find Dr. Louie waiting for him, and he almost walks out until Jimmy gently tells him to stay. Jerry and Dr. Louie are left alone in the living room. The gloves are off and words are not minced. Dr. Louie confronts Jerry with his behavior, indicating that Jerry seems to be using some kind of illegal drugs. Jerry denies all of it and says that his parents and grandparents put him up to this. Dr. Louie assures him that it is Jerry's behavior that put him in this situation and then, very calmly and gently, explains to him how his radical change in behavior indicates the influence of illegal drugs.

Finally, Jerry breaks down weeping and admits that taking a pill or two now and again is no big deal and helps him cope. Dr. Louie explains to him that this is not the right way to resolve personal issues. He explains to him that there are heathy and positive ways to resolve them, but not illegal drugs. Finally, he tells him that he needs professional help. Jerry finally agrees to speak further with Dr. Louie, without admitting that there is something wrong with him. The meeting lasts just over one hour.

Dr. Louie sets up an appointment at his office for the following day, after Jerry has finished school. The psychologist assures Jerry that neither his siblings nor anyone else, except for his parents, grandparents, and his good friend Fr. Nate will know about the meeting. Meanwhile, Jimmy, Jenny, Johnny, Josey, and Fr. Nate are praying their hearts out, asking the Lord to inspire Dr. Louie and move the heart and mind of Jerry to wake up to reality.

It takes four meetings for Jerry to admit that he has a problem. Dr. Louie assures him that he is there to help him confront and deal with his problems. At a certain stage in the therapy, Dr. Louie tells Jerry that he is doing very well and, as of that moment, he does not see any reason for Jerry to go to a rehabilitation clinic.

There are many good families in the world who try their very best to provide a wholesome upbringing for their children. Yet, this great dedicated effort does not guarantee that the child will not come to harm. A parent may provide the right tools, yet their child may choose not to use them. In this case, Johnny and Josey — like many parents in their situation — feel that they had done something wrong or had missed something very important. But this is far from truth because as a child matures physically, mentally, and emotional, he or she has to own up to his or her own personal decisions, mistakes, and consequences. In this regard, such parents must allow their growing child to be an adult and, therefore, personally accountable for good and bad decisions and behavior.

Good parents provide a religious upbringing for their children not only by what they say and teach, but also by what they do. Again, this religious upbringing does not automatically guarantee that the child will grow up into a person to whom religion and religious activities and values are part and parcel of life. Johnny and Josey have given a solid, wholesome, and religious upbringing to their son Jerry, but he had made some terrible mistakes and decisions. It is wrong for them to think that they have failed. Every person is expected to enter into a personal relationship with God and own up to his misdeeds.

Jerry's parents and grandparents remind us that the role of parents and grandparents in the upbringing of their child is essential, but it is no automatic guarantee that their young adult will hold on to the values received at home. No matter what, we must pray daily not only for the physical and emotional but also for the spiritual well-being of our children and grandchildren of any age.

A Rainbow Moment

Parents are often the last to realize that something major is wrong with their child, though all indications point to it. This is where good communication between parents and grandparents is essential; grandparents should feel free and comfortable to indicate to parents that something is amiss. It is also important to have a common and united understanding of when they should seek outside advice and help.

This family was right to turn to professionals for counsel and assistance. There is nothing shameful in doing so. Hiding behind shame and guilt resolves nothing; in fact, it takes great courage to seek other people's advice and assistance. In doing so, they encourage other families who may have family members with substance abuse problems to focus on the healing and recovery of their loved one and dismiss what might be thought or said by neighbors, coworkers, and parishioners.

If you or someone you care about find yourself facing such serious or similar problems, seek the help of our caring and loving God, and ask for His help. Don't lose hope, even in a severe trial. Even in dark times, God sends a rainbow, and so something amazing happens on our way to Heaven.

CHAPTER EIGHTEEN

Ongoing Adjustments

A Catholic Marriage, lived as a sacrament, is the means to holiness for both the spouses and for their family. Jimmy and Jenny know this firsthand. For many years their home has been the hub of many everyday activities that include their adult children and their young grandchildren. Jenny embodies what the Book of Proverbs says about a wife: "When one finds a worthy wife, her value is far beyond pearls. Her husband, entrusting his heart to her, has an unfailing prize. She brings him good, and not evil, all the days of her life."[176]

Married couples give and receive love, care, support, comfort, and a deep sense of security, not only for themselves but also for their children and grandchildren. The grandchildren keep them "young" and full of wonder. They share their joys and sorrows, their personal successes and failures, their leisure time, their anxious moments, their aggravations and anguish, and their sense of having achieved something. But there are also the years of education not only in academics but also in their Catholic beliefs and lifestyle — an education that involves the entire person. Jimmy and Jenny have seen their children grow into sound Catholic adults, get married, and have their own families, and they remain ready to help their children and grandchildren whenever the need arises. They also had shared and

---

[176] Prov. 31:10–12.

supported one another when their daughter Connie died so young. Jimmy and Jenny willingly assist in the recovery of their grandson Jerry and provide constant support and encouragement to Johnny and Josey when their son eventually needs to enter a rehabilitation clinic to recover, as well during his subsequent rare relapses.

Jimmy and Jenny have had some serious health issues over the years and have been thankful to have sailed through them; these medical challenges became opportunities to bring the entire family even closer. When Jimmy was suspected to have colon cancer, everyone was alarmed — then it turned out to be a false alarm. During the Covid-19 pandemic, the family remained in daily contact through Zoom and WhatsApp. They could hardly wait for the moment when all of them would again be able to gather at Jimmy and Jenny's home.

Judy, Jerry, and their younger brother Jeremy are away at college. Only Jolie, a junior in high school, is living in their parents' home. Initially both Johnny and Josey, as well as the grandparents, are apprehensive about Jerry living away from home. However, his rehabilitation has gone very well, and when the time arrives for him to go to college, he has been sober for three years and seems to be in control of his life. To the grandparents' and parents' great relief, Jerry does very well at college and has returned to the practice of the Catholic Faith without being pressed by anyone to do so.

Jimmy is retired and now stays home all the time. He and Jenny realize that they need to make some adjustments to their changing interpersonal dynamics. Jimmy's staying at home full-time provides Jenny with the opportunity to do something she really loves: going places with her granddaughters. Jimmy gets his turn with his grandsons.

One of the adjustments is Jimmy's early rising — something he has done for many years due to his work schedule. Now, still an early riser, he feels he has to do something and putters around the house to kill time. Furthermore, he tends to move things around the kitchen, though Jenny has always been in charge of this and had established a routine years ago. Jenny thinks that both of them should rise a little later and that, perhaps, he should not move things around in the kitchen because there is a good reason for each of the things to be in a specific place.

Another area of ongoing compromise and adjustment is the fact that Jimmy is getting hard of hearing and blasts the TV very early in the morning to listen to the news. Jenny must build up enough courage to very gently and delicately suggest to him that he needs to have his hearing checked. He does so a couple of days later and gets a hearing aid. One of the things that they love doing together is to go to the 7:00 a.m. Mass and take Fr. Nate out for breakfast three times a week.

One morning at breakfast, Fr. Nate asks Jimmy and Jenny if they might be willing to be involved in parish activities, now that Jimmy is retired. They could be involved as a couple and/or as individuals. He suggests the parish finance council, parish pastoral council, and the Order of Christian Initiation of Adults, usually called the OCIA. The latter would require attending diocesan classes for prospective instructors/catechists. There are two tracks available: a six-month intense course which entails two-hour morning classes three times a week, or a yearlong course with one three-hour class a week in the evenings. He tells them that this encompasses a real personal sacrifice and great personal commitment. But he emphasizes that being involved in the program is a real ministry as a catechist who would help in shaping the spiritual lives of many people and, in the long run, also help in the ministry of the Universal Church. Once either course is completed, there will be a paraliturgical ceremony of installation as a catechist at the cathedral. The program is geared toward prospective Catholics or those who need to complete the Sacraments of

Initiation. These candidates are required to attend weekly evening classes from the beginning of September until the end of Lent of the following year.

It does not take long for Jimmy and Jenny to inform Fr. Nate that they are interested in becoming a catechist couple and prefer to attend the six-month intensive course. He is delighted and tells them that he will put in the application the first chance he has because the intensive course is scheduled to begin at the end of that month, and they will be ready to assume their new role in the parish the following September.

When Jimmy and Jenny show up for the first catechist class, they are a little overwhelmed with all the information they are given, information flying at them like bullets out of a machine gun! However, during the break they discover that most of the rest of the class had the same feeling, and they begin to relax and form friendships in the group. Their classmates are wonderful, dedicated Catholics, full of fire to serve their respective parishes and God's people. So it is easy to bond. Meanwhile they adjust nicely to the way the course is being taught. In fact, after their initial apprehension, the entire course seems to go very fast. During one of their breakfast outings after Mass, Jimmy and Jenny are excited to tell Fr. Nate how they feel they are relearning their Catholic Faith and are more committed to it than ever. They always speak enthusiastically about the program.

Jimmy and Jenny are eager to tell the rest of the family about their classes, too. Subtly and diplomatically, Jimmy and Jenny begin to speak to their younger grandchildren about what they have learned at class that they think might interest the kids. The grandchildren in turn are inspired to see their ancient grandparents hitting the books and really studying and discussing various topics.

One of the major things that Jimmy and Jenny learn during the course is that the United States Bishops' Conference has made some changes to the Rite of Christian Initiation of Adults (RCIA) — including the name, which is now the Order of Christian Initiation for Adults (OCIA). The process has also been changed to reflect the differing backgrounds of those entering the program: some are seeking Baptism, whereas others are joining the Catholic Church from another Christian Creed or returning to the Catholic Church to complete the Sacraments of Initiation. For all, spiritual formation is an ongoing, lifelong process — those in the program will receive the sacraments when they are ready to do so, rather than when they have completed their time of instruction.

Jimmy and Jenny know from their personal experience that living as a committed Roman Catholic is a lifelong process of personal conversion. The new program means that the instructors are there not only to share the contents of the Catholic Faith but also to be actively involved with the candidates outside the classroom setting. In other words, they not only instruct, but also walk the faith journey with each candidate. Eventually, once Jimmy and Jenny are catechists, they begin realizing that they themselves are growing in the Faith in the company of the candidates. Thus, both the candidates and the instructions are having a very positive impact on Jimmy and Jenny.

Once the diocesan program is finished, Jimmy and Jenny go to the cathedral to be instituted in the ministry of catechists. Fr. Nate and their extended family are present, the entire ceremony is very moving, the bishop's words are very supportive and encouraging, and the spiritual challenge is set for Jimmy and Jenny. They are ready to witness more intensely their Catholic Faith and to share it with others — together, as a couple.

A Rainbow Moment

The faithful, lifelong service of couples like Jimmy and Jenny is a blessing both to the Church and to themselves. Through their actions as well as their simple presence, they demonstrate that the Sacrament of Marriage is one of the most important and intimate lifelong relationships and the bedrock for any society. And by remaining actively involved in the lives of their grown children and their growing grandchildren without interfering, meddling, or intruding, they give witness to the importance of family life. When storms arise, families join together to offer love, support, and encouragement.

As we age, life presents us with new opportunities to serve, learn, and grow. How we respond—with dignity and generosity, or by drawing inward and isolating ourselves—is vitally important. This new stage in life requires adjustments, more give and take, more sensitivity and patience, and a good dose of humor. And yet the sunset of our lives can still be very rewarding, very productive, and a great blessing to others. We are never too old to grow in faith. Therefore, here is another rainbow from God, for something amazing happens on our way to Heaven.

CHAPTER NINETEEN

Coping with Aging

JIMMY AND JENNY ARE now approaching their eighties. Five of their grandchildren have blessed them with twelve great-grandchildren. Each birth has given them a new shot in the arm. They are now busier, though it is obvious to everyone that their level of energy is gradually declining. They now have some health issues and need to rest more often.

Fr. Nate, their favorite pastor, has retired due to some major health issues; he now lives in an assisted living home. Jimmy and Jenny continue to visit him and have breakfast together three times a week, laughing together over past events. But as Fr. Nate's health continues to decline rapidly, they see themselves in him and ask themselves when their turn will arrive. He is younger than they by almost a decade, but much older in his personal suffering.

As the curtain of his life begins to close, Fr. Nate becomes increasingly expressive of his appreciation and love of Jimmy and Jenny, his steadfast friends of almost forty years. Jimmy and Jenny begin to prepare themselves for the day when God will call their friend to His heavenly home. They struggle greatly, feeling all over again the pain of losing their young Connie. Fr. Nate senses their struggles and tries to comfort them by thanking the Lord for his not-so-perfect but honest priestly ministry, and the blessing of his friendship with Jimmy and Jenny. There are times when they cry in their car as they drive back home. He tells them that he prays that one or two of their great-grandchildren might become a priest or a religious sister. They tell him that this is a wish for which they pray every day. He wants to know all about how their OCIA is coming along, about the candidates, and about their common journey in faith. Jimmy's and Jenny's faces brighten up, and their voices become very excited as they speak about the candidates and how the spiritual journey is going.

One morning as Jimmy and Jenny are visiting Fr. Nate, he kind of lets it slip that he thinks his time on earth is about to expire. There is a smile on his serene face, and his eyes seem to radiate light. On the other hand, Jimmy and Jenny try to encourage him by telling him that his time will be long in coming. After all, he is much younger than they are.

Fr. Nate can see their sorrow across their faces. They pray together. Then, one day, Fr. Nate ends their prayer of the Hail Mary in a way that is different from how he has always said it before: "Holy Mary, Mother of God, pray for me, a sinner, now and at the hour of my death. Amen." It is at this point that Jimmy and Jenny accept the fact that their beloved priest is about to die. They feel their eyes well up with tears, along with a resigned smile.

Fr. Nate falls asleep in the Lord later that day. Per Fr. Nate's instructions, the first persons called, even before the bishop is notified, are Jimmy and Jenny. They rush to the assisted living home to see their friend for the last time. They realize on the way there that Fr. Nate has gently prepared them for this moment of final separation.

Fr. Nate's funeral is huge. Johnny is one of the pall bearers and Jimmy is one of the readers at the Mass of Christian Burial. There is an overflowing crowd at the church. The bishop comments that Fr. Nate would have been very surprised with the turnout and with how many people he had touched with his ministry and how much he was loved. The bishop states that something original is about to happen at the request of Fr. Nate. The bishop informs the congregation that he will not deliver his own homily, for Fr. Nate had left one and asked that he read it at the Funeral Mass. Thus, the bishop opens a folder and begins reading:

"My dear people, at least I hope some of you are here for my Funeral Mass." The bishop stops for a few moments as sounds of chuckles come from the congregation. "I know that some of you will be thrilled to know that this is my last and shortest homily. It is so special that our great bishop is reading it on my behalf. I am sure that he will do a great job. And this way, he won't attempt to speak too highly of me, or 'canonize' me at my own Funeral Mass — giving a great shock to God, all of you, and even to me!"

There is more laughter and smiles from the people as the bishop observes: "Fr. Nate never lost his great sense of humor even while dying; he wrote this homily the day before the Lord called him." Taking up his notes again, the bishop continues reading. "You are gathered here to pray for me and to ask the Lord of Life to have mercy on my soul. Indeed, I am in dire need of that mercy because I am a poor sinner who is begging entrance at Heaven's doors. I have shared most of my life with many of you. Indeed, some of you have also shared most of your life with me as your unworthy priest. As I had come to know and to love you and minister to you and to your loved ones as your priest, you, too, had come to know me and shower me with your love. You accepted me as I was in my frailties, my limitations, my failures, my struggles, my shortcomings, my sorrow, my good days and my bad days, my joy, my success — or should I say more precisely God's success through my unworthy self, in my priestly youth, then middle age, and finally old age and retirement.

"I seek forgiveness from those whom I have offended in any way, shape, or form, and from those whom I have disappointed by falling short of their expectations. Please know that I was very energized by your acceptance, your assistance, your growth in the Faith, your celebrations of great moments in your lives, your exemplary humility, and your never-ending forgiveness. These, and many others, were the Lord's gifts to me through you … and they were overabundant and enriching. Each of you had a place in my heart and daily prayers. God shaped me through you as His servant. I am most grateful and thankful to Him and to you. The Lord has been with me throughout my priestly ministry, including when I was sick and frail, when I was dying. And he was with me when I died, and so I declare to you that Jesus is the Resurrection and the Life; whoever believes in Him, even when he dies, he shall live, for everyone who lives and believes in Him shall never die.[177] My soul lives and will be eventually reunited with my body on the Last Day, the day when the Lord will return in glory.[178]

"Finally, I ask of you three things: to allow the Lord to make you holy; to give your sons and grandsons to the Church to serve as priests of the High Priest, Jesus Christ, and to encourage your daughters and granddaughters to enter consecrated life; and to pray for the holiness of priests and religious. Please pray for me as I will beg the Lord to allow me to pray for you. Our physical separation is very brief in God's time. My journey of faith has ended. May yours be one full of spiritual growth and heavenly blessings, full of love, self-giving, prayers, and virtues. Thank you, my dear spiritual family. I thank God for giving you to me. I say farewell by borrowing the song from the lips of Our Lady, the Magnificat: My soul gives glory to the Lord and my spirit rejoices in God my Savior. Amen."

One could hear a pin drop as the bishop finishes Fr. Nate's words of farewell. There are many teary eyes. As the coffin is slowly being

---

[177] John 11:25–26.
[178] Matt. 16:27; 25:31; 1 Thess. 4:16.

led out of the church after Mass, the congregation explodes in spontaneous clapping. Through their tears and downcast faces, the people want to express their gratitude to God and love for Fr. Nate that morning. He spoke to them even in death, and many of those present begin thinking of how they want to live their lives in preparation to meet the Lord.

A Rainbow Moment

As we age, we are called upon with increasing frequency to say goodbye to cherished friends and family members whom God calls home. For the Catholic, *memento mori* (remember death) is a phrase spoken not with fear and dread, but with hope. It is a signal to evaluate our own lives and consider whether we need to change for the better, to cope better with our struggles, disappointments, frustrations, and failures, and begin seeing the need to appreciate more our blessings, many of which we have forgotten due to the vicissitudes of daily life. God delivers another one of His rainbows, for something amazing happens on our way to Heaven.

CHAPTER TWENTY

Sunset

THERE IS NEVER A convenient time for a loved one to die. Although Jimmy and Jenny are people of deep faith, they greatly miss Fr. Nate, almost as much as they still miss Connie. And yet they also know that God and their loved ones also want them to continue living, rather than to spend the rest of their days simply reminiscing. God has granted them time to serve and to love Him, His Church, and especially those in need.

At the same time, Jimmy and Jenny realize that their energy is steadily decreasing. Consequently, they must carefully discern — praying and seeking advice from their pastor and friends — about which activities and projects to undertake. They have recently hired a live-in helper and home companion, Corrie, who turns out to be a wonderful choice. Apart from the fact that Corrie does not drive, she practically does everything else around the house. Jimmy drives her to the supermarket and to anywhere else she needs to go, even during her time off. Jenny initially keeps a close eye on Corrie regarding her chores but becomes completely confident in her abilities within a month of Corrie moving in. Jimmy, Jenny, and their children soon begin considering Corrie as part of their family.

There is only one thing that silently bothers Jimmy and Jenny: although Corrie has been baptized and brought up as a Catholic, she no longer practices the Catholic Faith. She has never been married, and they are determined not to intrude into her private life. So, they decide to witness to Corrie by the way they live and the very gentle way they relate to her. Nevertheless, they pray daily for her return to the practice of the Catholic Faith.

Corrie instinctively knows that there is something very special about Jimmy, Jenny and their family, something she cannot pin down. But it is as concrete and real as the walls of her quarters in the house. She feels welcomed, respected, trusted, and loved. She says to herself that she must be doing something right. She has come to love the entire family — and admires how Jimmy and Jenny prioritize the time they spend with their extended family, especially the growing grandchildren and great-grandchildren. Their home is full of love, laughter, and little ones running around screaming and with very happy faces.

As Jimmy and Jenny continue to think about their parish involvement, they think that they should limit their involvement to continuing with the OCIA and walking the journey of faith with candidates in their parish as long as their declining health and energies allow. They are very much at peace with their decision. They never feel that they are useless and dispensable. Their view of life in old age goes against the world's trend toward a throwaway society and old people being viewed as a burden. They are most appreciative and grateful for every new moment and day the Lord allows them to have.

Corrie has been living with Jimmy and Jenny for about six months when, one day, she builds up enough courage to ask Jenny what she and Jimmy have been doing on Monday nights. Usually, men watch sports on television on those evenings, and this is not happening in that home.

Jenny silently thanks God for this inquiry and asks the Holy Spirit to illuminate her response. Smiling gently, Jenny tells Corrie that they are involved in the parish OCIA program, a parish program in which she and Jimmy journey with people who wish to become Catholic or those who wish to return to the Catholic Church. She does not want to overwhelm Corrie with too much information or to give her the impression that she and her husband expect Corrie to reactivate her participation in the Catholic Faith. On the other hand, Jenny feels that her and Jimmy's prayers for and witnessing to Corrie are working and thanks the Lord.

In the privacy of their bedroom that evening, Jenny is delighted to share this wonderful event with Jimmy, and he is thrilled. Their prayers for Corrie intensify and they leave the rest to Divine Providence. They do not have to wait long because the following Saturday afternoon Corrie asks Jenny if she could go with them to Mass the next day, Sunday. Jenny tells her that she and Jimmy would be honored by her presence. This is the first step for Corrie to return to practice her Catholic Faith. They take her to church that Sunday morning. They are deeply moved when they notice Corrie wiping a tear as she kneels during the Consecration.

Jimmy and Jenny continue to be very active grandparents, and Corrie enjoys preparing snacks for the grandchildren and great-grandchildren, playing with them, and helping cleaning up the mess after the little people leave their grandparents' home. Corrie cries when the youngest granddaughter, five years old, hugs her tightly and tells her: "I love you, Auntie Corrie." Corrie, crying, is certain then that she has found a loving home and family.

Jimmy and Jenny continue to provide their love and emotional support to their growing great-grandchildren, though they can no longer run after them, wrestle with them, or pick them up and bounce them around. Now they play board games with the older ones, and take the younger ones for a short ride to the local playground, watching them like hawks lest they get hurt or things begin to get out of hand. There are times when the grandparents say to the younger ones: "Sweetheart, I cannot do that. Perhaps you should ask Auntie Corrie." Corrie is most obliging.

However, Jimmy and Jenny never tire of teaching the little people, very simply, what being a Catholic means. They continue to be available to their grown children and grandchildren to provide them with counsel based on their long experience and acquired wisdom, but only when they ask. They continue to tell stories and share family and cultural traditions with the younger grandchildren. They go on teaching them limits and lessons, listening to their troubles and wiping away tears, and showing their grandchildren that they understand.

Of course, Jimmy and Jenny have to adapt to the new versions of "crises" in their grandchildren's lives. Now, children have electronic gadgets and social networks at their disposal that could put them at all kinds of risks; they experience more pressures to conform with the emerging self-centered and self-serving mentality. The older grandchildren face the social pressures of people their age: resisting the lure of opioids and other kinds of drugs; dealing with cultural confusion about sexual identity; and refusing to give in to pressure to become sexually active. As each new crisis arises, Jimmy and Jenny continue to offer sound, loving, and supportive advice, and continue to sustain an emotional connection with the younger ones. They are not only attentive to what the young ones are telling them but also to what is going in their social world, so full of tension and turmoil.

Jimmy and Jenny must also understand, address, and accept their growing vulnerability in many areas of their life as individuals and as a couple. Despite their ever-increasing medical expenses, the challenges of navigating a complex medical system, and the growing realization that they are now living in a world beyond their comprehension, they are determined to regard this time of their lives not as a burden but as a gift from God to spend their time together and with their loved ones.

Jimmy and Jenny still have their occasional disagreements, but they are careful that these not take away their happiness as individuals and as a couple. They have learned how to discuss their differences honestly, respectfully, and without feeling threatened. They know that they are there for one another, come what may. They also instinctively know that their faith plays a major part in their lives and that their prayer life keeps them persevering in the right perspective of their aging process and sense of mortality.

They have come to look at their personal life and marriage as if they were a tree. A tree has roots, needs ongoing nourishment, is always growing, is fruitful, shades people from the sun, and serves as a home to many, such as birds. Jimmy's and Jenny's roots are their love for God, the Church, one another, family, and friends. Their spiritual nourishment is their sacramental life, especially Holy Eucharist. Physically they are becoming more fragile, yet spiritually they continue to grow by journeying with the members of the OCIA program and staying close to family. And they delight in the fruit of this tree, especially in their happy home and extended, ever-growing family.

A Rainbow Moment

As we age and begin to face the normal changes of the aging process—a decline in energy, an increase in medical issues, and financial concerns included—we can choose to "circle the wagons" and isolate ourselves, or we can look for new ways to grow spiritually and relationally. We see an example of this with Jimmy and Jenny, who recognize their need for help and meet that need by welcoming Corrie into their home. How do you see this happening in your own family or community?

Corrie and their other friends find in Jimmy and Jenny a place to seek advice and comfort, and a place to find love. Even in old age, and even when facing our own challenges, God gives us opportunities to show His love to those around us. This is another one of God's rainbows, for something amazing happens on our way to Heaven.

CHAPTER TWENTY-ONE

Called to Glory

JIMMY AND JENNY ARE on their way to their family doctor for a regular checkup. Dr. Bob has been their doctor for decades. They feel very comfortable with him and think that he is genuinely concerned not only about their health but their overall well-being. So Jenny is very surprised when Dr. Bob tells her that he wants her to undergo some medical tests. Her blood pressure is erratic, and Jenny has an occasional dizzy spell and occasional shortness of breath. She thinks that this is normal for people her age and that she might have sometimes overdone things.

Dr. Bob is not so convinced. So he arranges for Jenny to get a couple of cardiovascular tests: a nuclear and echo test, a computerized tomography (CT) coronary angiogram, and possibly a coronary arteriography. Jenny and Jimmy are concerned, but decide to keep things to themselves until the results of the tests come in.

When the results are back, they are not encouraging. In fact, they are worrisome. Dr. Bob explains to them that Jenny is suffering from hypertension, congestive heart failure, and arrhythmia, particularly atrial fibrillation. Gently, Dr. Bob tells Jenny that she is running the risk of a stroke and has some serious heart issues. Jenny and Jimmy need a few minutes to digest this bad news, this real reminder of their mortality.

After somewhat recovering from the shock and whispering a prayer entrusting Jenny to God, Jimmy asks what should happen next. Dr. Bob tells them that they will first try medication.

They return home and decide to inform their children and Corrie the next morning. But that evening is rough. Jenny thinks that she could die any moment. Jimmy wonders if he might wake up the following morning, or any other morning, to find Jenny dead in bed beside him. Once again, they entrust everything into God's hands and ask Him to give them the grace of coping and to accept whatever He has planned for them. They also decide that beginning the next morning, they will stay in church after Mass and do the Stations of the Cross every day. They had done them every Friday during Lent, but now they will do them every day to remind themselves that their sufferings should be joined to that of the Lord, Who suffered so much for all of humanity. They end the day by praying what a priest prays at Night Prayer: "May the all-powerful Lord grant us a restful night and a peaceful death. Amen."

The next morning comes, and both wake up, though neither has slept well. They decide to offer that morning's Mass to seek inspiration from the Holy Spirit for the strength, peace, and wisdom to break the news to their children. Their grandchildren will be informed by their respective parents.

Jenny and Jimmy stay inside the church after Mass. They go to the middle of the church and pray devoutly the fourteen Stations of the Cross from where they are seated, without moving around. They do not ask for a healing miracle; rather, they ask for the grace to cope and to witness to the Lord through their personal mental, physical, and emotional sufferings. Jenny pictures Jesus looking at her during each Station and telling her: "This is what I did for you because I love you!"

Once they are back home, they have breakfast. Next, Jimmy calls each of their children, beginning with Johnny, their firstborn, and asks them to meet them there in the evening for dinner at 6:00 p.m. Corrie senses that there is something drastically wrong, but says nothing.

The children arrive, and all of them, including Corrie, have dinner together. Though the conversation is light and pleasant, they all sense an air of uneasiness in Jenny and Jimmy. After dessert and coffee are served, Jimmy tells them that they want to share with them some distressing news about their mother's health.

All eyes are on Jenny, but it is Jimmy who speaks. He tells them that their mother has had some dizzy spells and experienced some shortness of breath. So, he continues, they went to consult with Dr. Bob, who ordered a variety of tests. Jimmy, with his voice breaking, says that the news was bad. Jenny has some serious heart issues, but is being given some medication to see how things will go.

Silent tears drop from the eyes of the women, including Corrie's. The men are stoic. It is Jenny's turn to speak. She speaks of her and Jimmy's concerns and emphasizes that they are leaving everything in God's hands. She continues to say that her condition has made both her and Jimmy realize how very precious time is, that each moment is another gift from God, that she will slow down in her activities, and that she will rest more. She asks them to drop in whenever they can, with the grandchildren and the great-grandchildren. Jimmy concludes by telling his stunned family that they will leave it up to them to gently break the news to the grandchildren — the great-grandchildren are still babies. Having said this, he stops for a moment, and then they all break out crying. It is Jenny who pitches in and says that they are grateful to God for giving them a wonderful long life, a great family, and numberless blessings. As the family leave, each wiping tears, they kiss and embrace Jenny as if this is the last time they would see her alive. Corrie, inconsolable, goes to her quarters and sobs abundantly, though she takes precautions not to be heard.

When Jenny and Jimmy are finally alone, they are at peace and somewhat comforted by how things have gone. It is time for them to pray the Rosary. They decide to recite daily the Sorrowful Mysteries and seek the Lord's assistance. Next, they go to their bedroom and have a good night's rest.

✠   ✠   ✠

The next morning, fifteen minutes before Mass, they go to the sacristy and tell Fr. Frank, their pastor, of Jenny's condition. She asks to receive the Sacrament of the Anointing of the Sick, which he gives her on the spot. Jenny feels at peace.

Some three weeks later, Jenny tells Jimmy during dinner that she is not feeling well, is very tired, and wishes to retire to their bedroom. Jimmy becomes alarmed and asks her what she is feeling, if she has taken the medication, and if he should call Dr. Bob or take her to the hospital's emergency room. She complains about her left arm bothering her and has a great headache. She says she has taken the medication, and there is no need to bother Dr. Bob or go to the hospital. She says that a good night's sleep will work wonders for her. So, they go to their bedroom, recite the Rosary, and turn in, having prayed: "May the all-powerful Lord grant us a restful night and a peaceful death. Amen."

Around 3:00 a.m. the next morning, Jimmy wakes up suddenly. He turns to Jenny to see if she is still sleeping. He notices that she is not breathing. He tries to shake her gently, whispering her name, just to realize that she is gone. Her body is still warm. He takes her hand, and as he begins to cry, he has a massive stroke and dies quietly holding Jenny's hand.

✠   ✠   ✠

Corrie becomes concerned when neither Jenny nor Jimmy come down to go to church that morning. So, she goes to their bedroom to check on them, and knocks gently on the door. Having no response, she gingerly ventures in, and becomes hysterical when she realizes that both are dead. Though their faces look peaceful, she cannot stop shouting their names.

It takes her more than an hour to calm down. She calls Johnny, the eldest son, her hands shaking out of control and her voice very agitated. He tells her to immediately call for an ambulance and the police to come to his parents' home; he will alert the rest of the family. Corrie follows the instructions and makes the two calls. However, it is the coroner's car and not the ambulance that shows up with the police. The coroner calls Dr. Bob and asks him to come over.

The family is already there by the time Dr. Bob arrives. They are all in shock. They look at their parents, lovingly holding each other's hand and looking very peaceful. They are still crying when Dr. Bob arrives. He pronounces both of them dead and states that Jenny had suffered from very serious heart issues and that Jimmy had told him a few days before that he was having sharp chest pains, but he did not want to undergo tests until Jenny felt a little better. Dr. Bob diagnoses that Jimmy has died from a massive stroke. After examining closely the bodies, he states that Jenny probably had died around 2:45 a.m, and that Jimmy died soon thereafter, probably from discovering that Jenny had died. The coroner decides that there is no need for an autopsy. Dr. Bob signs the death certificate for both. They were inseparable in life and in death.

The news of their death travels very fast around the parish and at Jimmy's former work. Those who knew them all say how special the couple was. The phone begins to ring, and it is decided to leave it off the hook. Fr. Frank comes over to bless the deceased and comfort the family. He comments that Jenny and Jimmy truly lived the Sacrament of Marriage and touched the lives of many people. He blesses the bodies and says: "May the angels lead you to Paradise!"

Jimmy and Jenny were a living witness to the Lord's union with the Church. They grew old together in good times and in difficult times, in sickness and in health. Their marriage sustained them with the sacrament's grace. They inspired their children, grandchildren, and those who came to know them that marriage and family are truly gifts from God, that marital love grows and continues to grow even when the spouses get old and very sick, that sharing one's faith is a way of proclaiming the good news, and that in the end, a spouse is the other spouse's means of holiness. Thus, God has sent His last rainbow to Jimmy and Jenny, and something amazing happened on their way to Heaven.

A Rainbow Moment

The appearance of a rainbow indicates that harmony and peace among the elements have been restored.

Let us thank the Lord for sending us spiritual rainbows of grace during some very difficult moments throughout our lives.

Let us thank the Lord for sending these spiritual rainbows of grace to us in the heels of our rain of tears, crises, internal confusion, anxiety and perplexity. They grant us inner peace and hope.

Let us thank the gracious Lord for walking down the final spiritual rainbow in our life, taking us by the hand, and leading us up the bridge of the rainbow to His heavenly home.

About the Author

Msgr. Laurence Spiteri is a priest of the Archdiocese of Los Angeles, California, and serves as prelate auditor of the Roman Rota at the Vatican and commissioner of *ratum non consummatum* cases. He holds doctorates in biblical studies, psychology, canon law, and a specialization in international law regarding the Church-state relationship. He also serves as the official in charge of the legal office of the Vatican Apostolic Library, a voting member of the Historical Commission of the Dicastery of the Causes of Saints, an ad hoc judge at the Dicastery for the Doctrine of the Faith, a consultant to various Roman dicasteries and religious communities, and CEO of The Sanctuary of Culture Foundation, of the Treasures of History Foundation, and of the St. Joseph, Husband of Mary Foundation. He is a former associate director and judge at the Metropolitan Tribunal of Los Angeles; judge at the Tribunal of Las Vegas; assistant at the Apostolic Signatura; instructor in canonical procedures; and visiting professor of Sacred Scripture, Church History, History of Medieval Philosophy, and Catholic Theology in various academic institutions. He is the author of ninety-six books, some of which deal with canon and civil law, as well as ninety-three articles that appear in various professional publications. He has been published in various languages in the United States, England, Ireland, Malta, Mexico, Portugal, Italy, and Vatican City State.